dBASE III P·L·U·S™

THE POCKET REFERENCE

Miriam Liskin

Osborne **McGraw-Hill**
Berkeley, California

Osborne **McGraw-Hill**
2600 Tenth Street
Berkeley, California 94710
U.S.A.

For information on translations and book distributors outside of the U.S.A., please write to Osborne **McGraw-Hill** at the above address.

dBASE III PLUS™: The Pocket Reference

1234567890 SPCO 89876

ISBN 0-07-881305-0

CONTENTS

INTRODUCTION

This reference guide is a concise summary of the elements of the dBASE III PLUS command language. It is intended to serve as a reference for looking up the exact syntax of a command or for confirming which options are available. Although some usage suggestions and examples are included, this is not a learning guide. It assumes that you have some familiarity with dBASE III PLUS command syntax and the full-screen editing commands (such as APPEND and EDIT), and that you know how to navigate through the ASSIST menus and the full-screen editors used to define data bases, report and label forms, VIEWs, and QUERY files. Commands that are used primarily in dBASE III PLUS programs are marked with a square (▪).

DATA TYPES

dBASE III PLUS recognizes five data types for data base fields, four of which are also applicable to memory variables. These are the data types:

Character: any keyboard characters, including letters, numbers, and punctuation marks
Numeric: the digits 0 - 9 and, optionally, a decimal point and minus sign
Logical: the values "true" ("yes") and "false" ("no"), expressed as T, t, Y, y, F, f, N, and n
Date: calendar dates
Memo: variable-length fields for entering free-form text (not permitted for memory variables)

LIMITS AND SPECIFICATIONS

Record size: 128 fields and 4000 characters
File size: 1 billion records, 2 billion characters
Command length: 256 characters
Character strings: 256 characters
Numbers: 19 digits, 15 digits of accuracy
Memo fields: 5000 characters
Open files: 15 total, 10 data bases, 7 indexes per data base
Memory variables: 256 total, 31,000 characters
Index key: 100 characters
Index key expression: 220 characters

STANDARD FILE EXTENSIONS

dBASE III PLUS uses standard extensions to identify the different types of files it recognizes. You may override the default extensions, but if you assign a nonstandard extension to a file, you must type the complete file name, including extension, in every command that refers to the file.

CAT	Catalog data base file
DBF	Data base file
DBT	Data base text file (contains memo field text)
FMT	Format file
FRM	Report form file
LBL	Label form file
MEM	Memory variable file
NDX	Index file
PRG	Program or procedure file
QRY	Query file
SCR	Screen image file
TXT	Text file
VUE	View file

OPERATORS

Relational Operators:

Operator	Data Types	Meaning
=	C, N, D	Equal to
<> or #	C, N, D	Not equal to
>	C, N, D	Greater than
>=	C, N, D	Greater than or equal to
<	C, N, D	Less than
<=	C, N, D	Less than or equal to
$	C	Contained within

Logical Operators:

Operator	Data Types	Value of Resulting Expression
.AND.	L	.T. if both expressions linked are .T.
.OR.	L	.T. if either expression linked is .T.
.NOT.	L	.T. if following expression is .F.

Mathematical Operators:

Operator	Data Types	Meaning
+	N	Addition
	C	Concatenation
	D + N	Adds specified number of days to date
-	N	Subtraction
	C	Concatenation, embedded blanks combined at end
	D - N	Subtracts specified number of days from date
	D - D	Elapsed time between dates
*	N	Multiplication
/	N	Division
^ or **	N	Exponentiation

PRECEDENCE OF EVALUATION

Complex expressions are evaluated in the following order, unless you override the default by adding parentheses. Expressions containing parentheses are evaluated by working outward from the innermost set of parentheses.

Function evaluation
Exponentiation
Multiplication and division
Addition and subtraction
Character string concatenation
Evaluation of relational operators
Evaluation of logical operators:
.NOT.
.AND.
.OR.

FULL-SCREEN EDITING COMMANDS

dBASE III PLUS uses a similar set of cursor movement and editing command keys in all of its full-screen commands used to edit data (such as APPEND, EDIT, and BROWSE) and the editors used to create data bases and to edit memo fields and dBASE III PLUS programs. For most functions, there are both control key and keypad alternatives. The following table summarizes the commands and notes usage differences where they occur.

Control Key	Key	Function
Ctrl-E	Up Arrow	Move the cursor up one line
Ctrl-X	Down Arrow	Move the cursor down one line
Ctrl-D	Right Arrow	Move the cursor right one character
Ctrl-S	Left Arrow	Move the cursor left one character
Ctrl-F	End	Move the cursor right one field, column, or word
Ctrl-A	Home	Move the cursor left one field, column, or word
Ctrl-C	PgDn	Move forward to the next screen
Ctrl-R	PgUp	Move backward to the previous screen

Control Key	Key	Function
	Ctrl-PgUp or Ctrl-PgDn or Ctrl-Home	Enter the memo editor
	Ctrl-PgUp or Ctrl-End	Save the current memo field and exit the memo editor
Ctrl-B	Ctrl-Right Arrow	BROWSE: Pan the display right to display the next group of fields. Memo/Program Editors: Move the cursor to the end of the line
Ctrl-Z	Ctrl-Left Arrow	BROWSE: Pan the display left to display the previous group of fields. Memo/Program Editors: Move the cursor to the beginning of the line
Ctrl-G	Del	Delete the character at the cursor position
	Backspace	Delete the character to the left of the cursor
Ctrl-T		Delete characters from the cursor to the end of the word
Ctrl-Y		Delete characters from the cursor to the end of the line. Memo/Program Editors: Delete the line containing the cursor

Control Key	Key	Function
Ctrl-U		Mark the current record for deletion. CREATE/MODIFY Editors: delete the current field
Ctrl-V	Ins	Turn insert mode on (if it is off) or off (if it is on)
Ctrl-N		Insert a new line or field
Ctrl-Kb		Reformat the command or paragraph containing the cursor
Ctrl-Kf		Find a string of characters, searching forward from the cursor
Ctrl-Kl		Repeat the previous search
Ctrl-Kr		Read a disk file into the current memo field or program
Ctrl-Kw		Write the current memo field or program to another disk file
Ctrl-W	Ctrl-End	Save changes and exit
Ctrl-Q	Esc	Exit without saving changes
	F1	Turn help menu on (if it is off) or off (if it is on)
	Ctrl-Home	Access special option menus

COLOR AND MONOCHROME ATTRIBUTE CODES

The following codes are used in SET COLOR commands to symbolize the colors available on color monitors or attributes used on monochrome display screens:

Color:

Color	Low Intensity	High Intensity
Black	N	
Blue	B	B+
Green	G	G+
Cyan	BG	BG+
Red	R	R+
Magenta	RB	RB+
Brown	GR	
Yellow		GR+
White	W	W+
Blank	X	

Monochrome:

Attribute	Low Intensity	High Intensity
Light	W	W+
Dark	N	
Inverse	I	I+
Underlined	U	U+

READKEY( ) AND INKEY( ) VALUES FOR COMMAND KEYS

Command Key(s)	Readkey() no change	Readkey() data changed	Inkey()
Ctrl-S or Ctrl-H or Backspace or Left Arrow	0	256	19
Ctrl-D or Right Arrow	1	257	4
Ctrl-A or Home	2	258	1
Ctrl-F or End	3	259	6
Ctrl-E or Up Arrow	4	260	5
Ctrl-X or Down Arrow	5	261	24
Ctrl-R or PgUp	6	262	18
Ctrl-C or PgDn	7	263	3
Ctrl-Z or Ctrl-Left Arrow	8	264	26
Ctrl-B or Ctrl-Right Arrow	9	265	2
Ctrl-U	10	266	
Ctrl-N	11	267	
Ctrl-Q or Esc	12	268	
Ctrl-W or Ctrl-End	14	270	
Ctrl-M	15	271	
Return	16	272	
Home			29
End			23
Ctrl-Home	33	289	
Ctrl-PgUp	34	290	31
Ctrl-PgDn	35	291	30
Ins			22
Del			7
F1	36	292	

@ . . . SAY . . . GET FUNCTION SYMBOLS

The symbols listed below may be used in a FUNCTION clause in an @ . . . SAY . . . GET command to format or validate a field or memory variable as a whole. A function may also be included in a PICTURE clause. If the PICTURE contains both a function and a template, the function must come first, preceded by @ and followed by a single space.

Symbol	Data Types	Display/SAY	Edit/GET
C	N	Display CR (credit) after a positive number	None
D	N	Display DB (debit) after a positive number	None
(	N	Display a negative number in parentheses	None
B	N	Display a number left-justified	Display a number left-justified (data is stored right-justified)
Z	N	Display a zero value as blank (but including any decimal point)	Display a zero value as blank spaces (data is stored as 0)

Symbol	Data Types	Display/SAY	Edit/GET
D	C,N,D	Display in American date format (MM/DD/YY)	Display in American date format (storage format is determined by SET DATE option)
E	C,N,D	Display in European date format (DD/MM/YY)	Display in European date format (storage format is determined by SET DATE option)
A	C	None	Permit only alphabetic characters
!	C	Display data in uppercase	Convert entered data to all uppercase
R	C	None	Extra characters in a template are used for display only and do not become part of the data
Sn	C	Display the first n characters of the data	Scroll the data through a space n characters wide

@ . . . SAY . . . GET TEMPLATE SYMBOLS

The symbols listed below may be used in a PICTURE clause in an @ . . . SAY . . . GET command to format or validate a field or memory variable, one character at a time. Each symbol in the picture describes one character position in the variable being displayed or collected.

Symbol	Data Types	Display/SAY	Edit/GET
A	C	Display character unchanged	Permit only alphabetic character
X	C	Display character unchanged	Permit entry of any character
!	C	Display character in uppercase	Convert alphabetic character to uppercase
L	C	Display character unchanged	Permit only T,t,Y,y,F,f,N,n
	L	Display character unchanged	Permit only logical value
Y	L,C	Display character unchanged	Permit only Y,y,N,n
9	C	Display character unchanged	Permit only a numeric digit
	N	Display character unchanged	Permit numeric digit or minus sign

Symbol	Data Types	Display/SAY	Edit/GET
#	C	Display character unchanged	Permit numeric digit, space, minus sign, or decimal point
	N	Display character unchanged	Permit numeric digit, space, or minus sign
$	N	Display character if present, or a "$" in place of a space	None
*	N	Display character if present, or a "*" in place of a space	None
,	C	Display a "," if digit is present on both sides	Insert a "," into data
	N	Display a "," if digit is present on both sides	None
OTHER	C	Display symbol in place of data character. With R function, symbol is inserted into data field	Insert symbol into data. With R function, symbol is displayed only
	N	Symbol is inserted into data field	None

SYNTAX NOTATION AND ABBREVIATIONS

This guide uses the same standard notation as the dBASE III PLUS manual. UPPERCASE is used for all dBASE III PLUS keywords (words that are recognized by dBASE III PLUS as part of its command vocabulary), including command verbs, function names, words like FOR, WHILE, and TO, which introduce command clauses, and command options like OFF or DELIMITED. You may type keywords in any combination of uppercase and lowercase.

Optional command components are enclosed in square brackets ([]). When you use these options, remember not to type the brackets.

Two options are separated by a slash (/) if one or the other, but not both, may be used in a command. Many of the SET options have two allowable values (in most cases, ON or OFF); the default status of these options is printed in UPPERCASE, with the alternate value in lowercase. For example, the command to turn the terminal's beeper on or off is written as SET BELL ON/off.

Substitutions are printed in *lowercase italics* and enclosed in angle brackets (<>). When you use these commands, do not type the brackets or the exact words printed between the brackets; instead, you should make the appropriate substitution. For example, the command to create a new data base is listed as CREATE <*file name*>. To use this command to create a mailing list database called MAILLIST, you would type CREATE MAILLIST.

All dBASE III PLUS commands consist of a verb, and, optionally, one or more additional keywords or clauses. Command words (but *not* function names) may be abbreviated, provided that the portion of the command word you type is at least four characters long; if you include more than four characters, they must all be correct. For example, DELIMITED may be abbreviated to DELI or DELIM, but not DELIT.

In most cases, dBASE III PLUS command clauses and options may be used in any combination and typed in almost any order. The order used in the command summary in this guide was chosen so that the commands would read as much like English sentences as possible.

The following terms are used to describe the substitution items:

alias: An optional alternate name for a data base, which may be up to ten characters long and may contain an embedded underscore (_). The alias is specified in the USE command that opens the file; if you do not assign an alias, dBASE III PLUS assigns the file name as the alias. Some commands require that you use the alias rather than the file name if the two are different.

alias->field: A field in a data base open in a work area other than the currently selected work area.

character string: Any sequence of characters, enclosed in single quotes ('), double quotes ("), or square brackets ([]).

column: A screen or printer column (horizontal) coordinate. Columns are numbered from left to right, beginning with 0.

condition: A logical expression that evaluates to .T. or .F.

current: Used to describe the disk drive and subdirectory from which dBASE III PLUS was loaded, the selected work area, the data base file open in the selected work area, or the record at the position of the dBASE III PLUS record pointer.

drive: A disk drive designator (A, B, C, etc.), followed by a colon (:) if it forms part of a file name.

exp: Any syntactically valid dBASE III PLUS expression composed of data base fields, memory variables, functions, constants, and operators.

expC: An expression that evaluates to a character string.

expD: An expression that evaluates to a date.

expL: An expression that evaluates to a logical value (.T. or .F.).

expN: An expression that evaluates to a number.

field: The name of a field in the data base open in the currently selected work area.

file name: A valid MS-DOS file name. You must include the disk drive if the file does not reside on the default drive, and specify the full path name if the file is not in the current subdirectory (unless you have used a SET PATH command to specify a search path for files not in the current subdirectory). Any command that manipulates a particular type of file (for example, USE, which opens a data base file, or SAVE, which creates a memory variable file) assumes the standard dBASE III PLUS extension unless you override it by explicitly typing the extension. Commands that may operate on any type of disk file (for example, ERASE or RENAME) must always include the extension.

key or **key expression:** The expression used as the basis for indexing or sorting a data base file.

list: One or more items of the same type (fields, files, expressions, indexes, etc.) separated by commas.

memvar: A memory variable.

n: A number.

path: A DOS path name (the path through the subdirectory structure from the current subdirectory to the specified file) followed by a backslash (\).

row: A screen or printer row (vertical) coordinate. Rows are numbered from top to bottom, beginning with 0.

scope: The range of records in a data base to be acted on by a command. The valid scopes are:

ALL	The entire file.
NEXT <*expN*>	A number of records equal to the value of *expN*, including the current record.
RECORD <*expN*>	A single record; its record number is the value of *expN*.
REST	All of the records from the record (including the current record) to the end of the file.

In interpreting the *scope*, dBASE III PLUS takes into consideration any factors that affect the sequence or the range of records to be processed, including indexes, FILTERs, and the status of the DELETED option. For example, with a FILTER in effect and DELETED ON, ALL means all records not marked for deletion and that satisfy the FILTER condition.

skeleton: A pattern of letters and wildcard symbols that a file or variable name must match. The two wildcard characters are ?, which stands for any single character, and *, which substitutes for any combination of characters.

variable: Either a memory variable or a data base field.

COMMAND SYNTAX SUMMARY

▪ ▶ ?/?? [<*exp list*>]

Displays (if CONSOLE is ON) and/or prints (if PRINT is ON) the expressions in *exp list*, each pair separated by a single space. ? first issues a carriage return and line feed and thus displays or prints the expressions on the next available line. ?? displays the listed expressions beginning at the current cursor position (on the screen) or the current print head position. When no expressions are listed, ? displays or prints a blank line.

▪ ▶ @ . . . SAY . . . GET

@ <*row*>,<*column*>
[[SAY <*exp*> [PICTURE <*picture*>]
[FUNCTION <*function*>]] [GET <*variable*>
[PICTURE <*picture*>] [FUNCTION
<*function*>] [RANGE <*exp*>, <*exp*>]]]

- **@ <*row*>,<*column*> [CLEAR]**
- **@ <*row1*>,<*column1*> [CLEAR] TO <*row2*>,<*column2*> [DOUBLE]**

@ . . . SAY . . . GET commands are used in format files and in dBASE III PLUS programs to display or print text and data at specific positions on the screen or page. *Row* and *column* may be any valid numeric expressions representing screen or printer coordinates. For the screen, *row* must be between 0 and 24, and *column* must be between 0 and 79. For the printer, both *row* and *column* may range from 0 to 255, provided that lower limits are not imposed by the printer itself.

If a SAY clause is included, the specified expression is displayed on the screen with the *standard* display attributes (if you have SET DEVICE TO SCREEN) or printed (if you have SET DEVICE TO PRINT) at the designated row and column coordinates. Data may be placed on the screen in any order, but printing must proceed from left to right on each line and from top to bottom on each page.

If a GET clause is included, the specified expression is displayed on the screen with the *enhanced* display attributes (if you have SET DEVICE TO SCREEN). If you have SET DEVICE TO PRINT, GET commands are ignored.

If a PICTURE and/or FUNCTION clause are included, the *function* and/or *picture* are used to validate and format data displayed by a SAY clause or collected by a GET clause.

If a RANGE clause is included, it specifies the permissible range of values for a numeric or date field. The two *exp*'s in the RANGE clause may be any valid numeric or date expressions (depending on the type of data being collected). The RANGE clause allows the user to press ENTER to leave any existing value unchanged, but, if new data is entered, the cursor will not advance to the next item unless the value is within the allowable range.

@ . . . SAY . . . GET commands may be combined into a format file to draw a custom input screen for a data base. The format file may be invoked with SET FORMAT TO *<format file name>* and used to draw the screen for APPEND, EDIT, CHANGE, and INSERT. A format file may also be invoked, to edit a single record, with READ. READ commands within a format file create multipage screens.

In a program, one or more @ . . . SAY . . . GET commands *must* be followed by a READ in order to allow the user to edit the data. Memo fields may be accessed with @ . . . SAY . . . GET only if the command is part of a format file used with APPEND or EDIT (not activated by a READ).

@ ***<row>,<column>*** erases the specified row, beginning at the specified column.

@ ***<row>,<column>* CLEAR** erases a rectangular area of the screen; the *row* and *column* coordinates specify the upper left corner of the area.

@ ***<row1>,<column1>* TO *<row2>,<column2>*** draws a continuous single-line box on the screen or a double-line box (if the keyword DOUBLE is included). The two sets of row and column coordinates specify the upper left and lower right corners of the box. If the two row coordinates are the same, a horizontal line is produced; if the two column coordinates are identical, a vertical line results.

@ ***<row1>,<column1>* CLEAR TO *<row2>,<column2>*** erases a rectangular region on the screen; the upper left corner has the coordinates *row1* and *column1*, and the lower right corner has the coordinates *row2* and *column2*.

▪ ACCEPT [<*expC*>] TO <*memvar*>

Collects input from the user and creates the character string memory variable *memvar* to store the input. If *expC* is included, it is displayed as a prompt. If the user presses ENTER without typing anything else, *memvar* will be a null character string of length zero.

APPEND

▪ APPEND BLANK

APPEND FROM <*file name*> [FOR <*condition*>] [TYPE DELIMITED [WITH <*delimiter*>/BLANK]/SDF/DIF/SYLK/WKS]

APPEND adds new records to the current data base, using the standard dBASE III PLUS full-screen editing commands. Pressing PgUp allows you to edit existing records; however, these records are displayed in sequential order even if the data base was opened with an index.

APPEND BLANK adds a blank record to the current data base and positions the record pointer to the new record without invoking the full-screen edit mode. Usually, the fields are filled in with REPLACE or GET commands.

APPEND FROM adds records from the named file to the current data base. If a *condition* is specified, it must refer only to fields that are common to both data bases. Unless you have SET DELETED ON, records that have been marked for deletion are APPENDed and are not marked as deleted in the file that receives the data. Data is transferred between two DBFs by matching identically named fields.

If the SDF ("System Data Format") option is specified, the file from which records are APPENDed is assumed to be a fixed length text file with a carriage return at the end of each record.

If the DELIMITED option is specified, the file from which records are APPENDed is assumed to be a text file in which the fields are separated by commas, with a carriage return at the end of each record. If character fields in the text file are surrounded with any delimiters other than double quotes, the delimiter must be specified in the WITH clause. If DELIMITED WITH BLANK is selected, the fields are assumed to be separated by single spaces.

When dBASE III PLUS APPENDs data from DIF ("Data Interchange Format"), SYLK (Multiplan "Symbolic Link"), and WKS (Lotus Worksheet) files, rows in the spreadsheet become records in the data base, with each column supplying data for a field.

In all variations of the APPEND command, any indexes opened together with the data base are updated to account for the new records.

ASSIST

Invokes a menu-driven mode of operation for dBASE III PLUS.

AVERAGE [<*scope*>] [<*expN list*>] [FOR <*condition*>] [WHILE <*condition*>] [TO <*memvar list*>]

Calculates the average value for each expression in the list for the range of records in the current data base defined by the *scope* and *conditions*. If no expressions are listed, all numeric fields are AVERAGEd. If no *scope* is specified, ALL is assumed. If you have SET TALK ON, the averages are displayed on the screen, and if you have SET HEADING ON, the *expressions* are displayed above the results. If a list of memory variables is included, the named numeric variables are created to store the averages.

BROWSE [FIELDS <*field list*>] [LOCK <*expN*>] [FREEZE <*field*>] [WIDTH <*expN*>] [NOFOLLOW] [NOMENU] [NOAPPEND]

Enters a full-screen edit mode in which records are displayed one per line, with the fields aligned in columns. The first record displayed is the current record. You may not display or edit memo fields using BROWSE. Any data displayed on the screen may be edited; records may be deleted or recalled with CTRL-U; and new records may be added (just as in EDIT) by positioning the record pointer to the last record and then pressing PgDn.

If a FIELDS clause is included, only the named fields are displayed, in the specified order. If the LOCK clause is included, *expN* specifies the number of fields that remain fixed on the left side of the screen. If the FREEZE option is included, editing is restricted to the specified field, although you may still pan the display left or right to view the entire record. If the WIDTH option is included, *expN* specifies the maximum display width for any field; the data scrolls left and right within this width so you can edit the entire field.

The NOFOLLOW option controls the position of the record pointer after the key field is changed in a data base opened with an index. Normally, the record pointer remains positioned at the same record after you change the index key field, and the screen is redrawn with this record at the top. Because the record has moved in the index, a different set of records will occupy the screen after the change. NOFOLLOW causes the record pointer to be repositioned to the record originally displayed below the one that was changed, so that the screen display remains constant except for the disappearance of the altered record.

The NOAPPEND option prevents records from being added to a data base from within BROWSE.

LOCK and FREEZE may also be set from the BROWSE option menu invoked by pressing Ctrl-Home. This menu also contains commands to GOTO the TOP or BOTTOM of the file or to a particular record, specified by number, or to carry out a SEEK command if the file was opened with an index; the menu is not accessible if the NOMENU option is included in the BROWSE command.

▪ ▶ CALL <*module name*> [WITH <*expC*>]

Executes a binary program file loaded into memory with the LOAD command. The value of *expC* is passed to the program as a parameter. LOAD and CALL should be used only for subroutines written expressly to be executed this way; COM or EXE files (including most commercial software) should be invoked with the RUN command instead.

▪ ▶ CANCEL

Causes dBASE III PLUS to exit immediately from the currently running program, close all open program files (but not a procedure file, if one is open), and return to the dot prompt.

▶ CHANGE [<*scope*>] [FIELDS <*field list*>] [FOR <*condition*>] [WHILE <*condition*>]

Enters a full-screen mode to edit the specified fields in the range of records defined by the *scope* and *conditions.* If no *scope* is specified, ALL is assumed. CHANGE is identical to EDIT.

► CLEAR ALL/FIELDS/GETS/ MEMORY/TYPEAHEAD

CLEAR erases the screen, leaving the cursor positioned in the upper left corner, and CLEARs all pending GETs.

CLEAR ALL closes all data base files, indexes, format files, and CATALOG files in all of the ten work areas, selects work area 1, and releases all memory variables.

CLEAR FIELDS cancels a field list established with SET FIELDS TO <*field list*>, and turns off the field list as if you had typed SET FIELDS OFF.

- **CLEAR GETS** cancels all pending GETs, preventing the user from editing any variables that have not yet been collected by a READ. You may not issue more GET commands than specified by the GETS option in CONFIG.DB (128 if you have not changed the default) between CLEAR GETS, CLEAR, or READ commands.

- **CLEAR MEMORY** releases all memory variables, both PUBLIC and PRIVATE.

- **CLEAR TYPEAHEAD** deletes all characters in the typeahead buffer.

▪ ▶ CLOSE ALL/ALTERNATE/ DATABASES/FORMAT/INDEX/ PROCEDURE

Closes all files of the specified type.

CLOSE ALTERNATE (exactly like SET ALTERNATE [TO]) closes the current alternate file.

CLOSE DATABASES closes all data bases, indexes, and format files in all ten work areas, except a CATALOG file open in work area 10.

CLOSE FORMAT (exactly like SET FORMAT [TO]) closes the format file in the current work area.

CLOSE INDEX (exactly like SET INDEX [TO]) closes all index files in the current work area.

▪ **CLOSE PROCEDURE** (exactly like SET PROCEDURE [TO]) closes the current procedure file.

▶ CONTINUE

Searches the current data base, starting with the current record, for the next record that satisfies the condition in the most recent LOCATE command and leaves the data base positioned at the matching record. If you have SET TALK ON, the record number is displayed. If no matching record is found within the *scope* specified in the LOCATE command, an "End of locate scope" message is displayed.

COPY TO *<file name>* **[***<scope>***] [FIELDS** *<field list>***] [FOR** *<condition>***] [WHILE** *<condition>***] [TYPE DELIMITED [WITH***<delimiter>***/BLANK]/SDF/DIF/ SYLK/WKS]**

COPY FILE *<file 1>* **TO** *<file 2>*

COPY STRUCTURE TO *<file name>* **[FIELDS** *<field list>***]**

COPY TO *<file name>* **STRUCTURE EXTENDED**

Copies the range of records from the current data base defined by the *scope* and *conditions* to a new file. This file is created by the COPY command or deleted and recreated if it already exists. Records that have been marked for deletion are COPYed unless you have SET DELETED ON. If no *scope* is specified, ALL is assumed. If a *field list* is included, only the named fields are COPYed, in the specified order; otherwise, the new file has the same structure as the original.

If the SDF option is specified, COPY creates a text file consisting of fixed length records with a carriage return at the end of each record instead of a DBF.

If the DELIMITED option is specified, COPY creates a text file in which the fields are separated by commas, with a carriage return at the end of each record. If a *delimiter* is included, the specified punctuation mark is used to surround character fields instead of the default double quotes. If DELIMITED WITH BLANK is selected, the fields are separated by single spaces, with no punctuation surrounding character fields.

When dBASE III PLUS COPYs data to DIF ("Data Interchange Format"), SYLK (Multiplan "Symbolic Link"), and WKS (Lotus Worksheet) files, records in the data base become rows in the spreadsheet, with each field supplying data for one column and the field names entered into the spreadsheet as column titles.

COPY STRUCTURE creates an empty data base file containing the fields listed in the *field list* in the specified order or all of the fields in the current file if no *field list* is given.

COPY TO *<file name>* STRUCTURE EXTENDED creates a structure-extended file that describes the structure of the current file (instead of creating a data base with the same structure). The *structure-extended file* is a data base that has one record for each field in the current file, with four fields, named FIELD_NAME, FIELD_TYPE, FIELD_LEN, and FIELD_DEC, that contain the names, types, lengths, and number of decimal places of the fields. This file may be edited with MODIFY STRUCTURE, if necessary, and used to create a new data base with the CREATE FROM command.

COPY FILE *<file 1>* TO *<file 2>* creates a copy of *file 1* under the name *file 2*. Any disk file may be copied with this command, so the extension (and path, if the file is not in the current subdirectory) must be included.

▶ COUNT [<*scope*>] [FOR <*condition*>] [WHILE <*condition*>] [TO <*memvar*>]

Counts the number of records in the current data base in the range defined by the *scope* and *conditions*. If no *scope* is specified, ALL is assumed. If you have SET TALK ON, the count is displayed on the screen. If a memory variable is included, the named numeric variable is created to store the count.

▶ CREATE <*file name*>

CREATE <*file name*> FROM <*structure-extended file*>

Enters a full-screen mode in which you create a new data base file by defining names, types, lengths, and, for numeric fields, number of decimal places, for up to 128 fields, totaling up to 4000 bytes. If you do not specify the *file name*, dBASE III PLUS will prompt you to enter it.

If you include the FROM option, the structure of the new file is determined by the contents of the structure-extended file. This file is a data base that has one record for each field in the structure it describes, with four fields, named FIELD_NAME, FIELD_TYPE, FIELD_LEN, and FIELD_DEC, that contain the names, types, lengths, and number of decimal places of the fields. The file is usually generated with a COPY command using the STRUCTURE EXTENDED option, but it may be defined with CREATE, provided that you adhere to the four standard field names that allow dBASE III PLUS to recognize the data base as a structure-extended file.

▶ CREATE LABEL *<label file name>*

Creates a new label form or edits an existing form in a menu-driven environment. If you do not specify the *file name*, dBASE III PLUS will prompt you to enter it. If no data base is open in the selected work area, you will be prompted to enter it as well. This command is identical to MODIFY LABEL.

To specify the size and shape of the labels, you first select one of five predefined formats. If necessary, you may then change the label width (1 to 120 characters), label height (1 to 16 lines), left margin (0 to 250 characters), number of labels across the page (1 to 15), lines between labels (0 to 16 lines), and spaces between labels (0 to 120 characters) if you are printing more than one across.

For each line on the label, you may specify as the contents any valid dBASE III PLUS expression up to 60 characters long. If more than one data base is open, you may print fields from any open file by referring to all fields in unselected work areas as *alias->field name*.

▶ CREATE QUERY *<query file name>*

Creates a new query file or edits an existing file in a menu-driven environment. If you do not specify the *file name*, dBASE III PLUS will prompt you to enter it. If no data base is open in the selected work area, you will be prompted to enter it as well. This command is identical to MODIFY QUERY.

You may enter up to seven separate conditions linked with the logical operators .AND., .OR., and

.NOT. and grouped ("nested") with parentheses. If more than one data base is open, you may include fields from any open file, provided that you have specified the fields to be accessed with a SET FIELDS command or opened a VIEW that includes a field list.

The selection criteria stored in the query file are placed in effect with SET FILTER TO FILE *<query file name>*.

▶ CREATE REPORT *<report file name>*

Creates a new report form or edits an existing form in a menu-driven environment. If you do not specify the *file name*, dBASE III PLUS will prompt you to enter it. If no data base is open in the selected work area, you will be prompted to enter it as well. This command is identical to MODIFY REPORT.

To specify the overall page layout for the report, you may enter up to four page title lines of up to 60 characters each, the page width (1 to 500 characters), left and right margins, and number of lines per page (1 to 500). There are options to double space the report, to issue a form feed command to the printer before and/or after printing the report, and to print the report "plain" (without page numbers, date, or page titles).

You may print one or two levels of subtotals and specify the text to be printed at the beginning of each group of records as a *group* or *subgroup heading*. It is your responsibility to ensure that the data base is sorted or indexed on the same expression that defines the subtotal breaks. You can choose to print a summary-only report that includes only the subtotals and grand totals, with no detail records.

For each column on the report, you may specify as the contents any valid dBASE III PLUS expression up to 254 characters. If more than one data base is open, you may print fields from any open file by referring to all fields in unselected work areas as *alias–>field name*. You may specify up to four lines of column titles, the width of the column, and, for numeric fields, the number of decimal places and whether or not to accumulate totals and subtotals for the column.

▶ CREATE SCREEN *<screen file name>*

Creates a new screen form or edits an existing form in a menu-driven environment. If you do not specify the *file name*, dBASE III PLUS will prompt you to enter it. You can select a data base file to provide the fields displayed or collected on the screen, or you can create a data base at the same time you draw the screen image. This command is identical to MODIFY SCREEN.

To define the screen image, you type background text directly on a "blackboard" and define the locations where fields are displayed or collected. For each field, you may also specify a PICTURE, FUNCTION, or RANGE to format or validate the data. Boxes and lines consisting of the single- and double-lined graphics characters may also be included on a screen.

The screen image is saved in two ways — an SCR file that stores the screen image for subsequent editing and an FMT file that draws the input screen for the APPEND, EDIT, CHANGE, and INSERT commands when the format file is invoked with SET FORMAT TO *<format file name>*.

▶ CREATE VIEW *<view file name>* [FROM ENVIRONMENT]

Creates a new view file or edits an existing file in a menu-driven environment. If you do not specify the *file name*, dBASE III PLUS will prompt you to enter it. This command is identical to MODIFY VIEW.

To define the view, you first select one or more data bases, each of which may be opened with one or more indexes. You may also define how to link the files with SET RELATION, specify the list of fields that may be accessed, and, optionally, specify a format file and filter condition.

If the FROM ENVIRONMENT clause is included, the view is created based on the files and indexes currently open and the relations, field list, format file, and filter condition currently in effect.

The files are opened, and the relationships among them that are defined in the view file are placed in effect with SET VIEW TO *<view file name>*.

▶ DELETE [<*scope*>] [FOR <*condition*>] [WHILE <*condition*>]

Marks for deletion the records in the current data base in the range defined by the *scope* and *conditions*. If no *scope* is specified, only the current record is DELETEd. Records marked for deletion are physically removed from the file, and the space they occupy is released only when you PACK the data base. Records marked for deletion may be recovered with the RECALL command until a file is PACKed.

You may SET DELETED ON to cause dBASE III PLUS to ignore deleted records except when explicitly accessed by record number. If you have SET DELETED OFF, deleted records are identified by an asterisk (*) next to the record number in LIST or DISPLAY commands and by the "*Del*" indicator in the Status Bar (or on the top line of the screen if you have SET STATUS OFF) in the full-screen edit modes.

▶ DELETE FILE <*file name*>

This command is identical to ERASE.

▶ DIR [<*drive*>:] [<*path*>] [<*skeleton*>] [TO PRINT]

Displays a directory of the specified files. If no *drive*, *path*, or file name *skeleton* is specified, only data base files are listed, and the display includes for each file the number of records, date of last update, and file size. If a *drive*, *path*, or file name *skeleton* is included, files are displayed four across, much like the listing produced by adding the /W (wide) option to an MS-DOS DIR command. Even with a SET PATH command in effect, only files from the current subdirectory are displayed if no *path* is specified.

▶ DISPLAY [<*scope*>] [<*exp list*>] [FOR <*condition*>] [WHILE <*condition*>] [TO PRINT] [OFF]

Displays the specified expressions for the range of records in the current data base defined by the *scope* and *conditions*. If no *scope* is specified, only the current record is displayed, and with no *exp list*, all fields are included. The display pauses every 20 lines to allow you to read the screen; pressing any key displays the next group of 20 lines. If you have SET HEADING ON, the listed *expressions* are displayed as column titles in the same mixture of uppercase and lowercase used in the DISPLAY command.

The contents of memo fields are displayed only if the field names are explicitly included in the *exp list*. TO PRINT causes dBASE III PLUS to echo the screen display to the printer. OFF suppresses the display of the record numbers. The DISPLAY command is similar to LIST, except that LIST assumes a default *scope* of ALL and does not pause every 20 lines.

DISPLAY FILES [LIKE <*skeleton*>] [TO PRINT]

This command is identical to DIR, except that the optional TO PRINT phrase causes dBASE III PLUS to echo the screen display to the printer.

DISPLAY HISTORY [LAST <*expN*>] [TO PRINT]

Displays a list of the commands in history, normally 20 unless you have increased this number with a SET HISTORY command. TO PRINT causes dBASE III PLUS to echo the screen display to the printer. If the LAST clause is included, *expN* specifies the number of commands displayed, which are taken from the bottom of the list. Every 16 lines the display pauses to allow you to read the screen; pressing any key displays the next group of 16 lines.

DISPLAY MEMORY [TO PRINT]

Displays all active memory variables. The display pauses when the screen is full; pressing any key displays the next screenful of variables. TO PRINT causes dBASE III PLUS to echo the screen display to the printer. For each variable, the display includes the name, status (PUBLIC or PRIVATE), data type, stored value, the program (if any) that created the variable, and, for numeric variables, the display value (which may include fewer decimal places than the stored value).

At the end of the display, dBASE III PLUS

summarizes the number of variables defined, the number of bytes they occupy, the number of remaining variables (256 minus the number already defined), and the number of bytes remaining (the value of MVARSIZ, which is 6000 bytes unless you have increased it with an entry in CONFIG.DB, minus the number already used). This command is similar to LIST MEMORY, except for the pause after filling the screen.

► DISPLAY STATUS [TO PRINT]

Displays the current status of the working environment, with a pause between screens to allow you to read the display. TO PRINT causes dBASE III PLUS to echo the screen display to the printer.

For each currently active work area, dBASE III PLUS displays the open data base, all index file names and index key expressions, the file alias, the name of the DBT file if the data base contains memo fields, the name of any open format file, the FILTER condition if one is in effect, and any RELATION used to link the file to another data base. In a network environment, the display includes any file locks currently in effect and a list of any records currently locked.

The display also includes the file search path, default disk drive, selected printer port, left margin for printouts, the currently selected work area, the status of most of the options controlled by SET commands, and the function key assignments. This command is similar to LIST STATUS, except for the pauses between screens.

DISPLAY STRUCTURE [TO PRINT]

Displays the structure of the current data base file. The display pauses after every 16 fields; pressing any key displays the next 16 fields. TO PRINT causes dBASE III PLUS to echo the screen display to the printer. For each field, the display includes the name, data type, length, and, for numeric fields, number of decimal places. If a field list is in effect, the fields specified in the SET FIELDS commands are marked with a ">". dBASE III PLUS also displays the number of records in the file, the date of last update, and the total record length (the sum of the field lengths plus the one character used for the deletion marker). This command is similar to LIST STRUCTURE, except for the pause every 16 fields.

DISPLAY USERS

In a network environment, displays a list of the network workstation names of the users currently logged onto dBASE III PLUS, with the currently logged user marked with a "<".

DO *<program name>* [WITH *<parameter list>*]

Runs the specified dBASE III PLUS program or calls the named procedure, if a procedure file is open. (If a procedure in the open procedure file has the same name as a program, the procedure will be executed.) When the program or procedure terminates, control returns to the line in the calling program that follows the DO command or to the dot prompt if the DO command was executed from the dot prompt.

If a *parameter list* is included, the listed expressions are passed to the called program, which must contain a PARAMETERS command with the same number of parameters. The correspondence between the parameters in the DO command in the calling program and the PARAMETERS command in the called program or procedure is established by the order in which they are listed. The parameters may include any valid dBASE III PLUS expressions, but if fields are passed as parameters, the file alias must be specified, even for fields in the currently selected work area. All changes made to the values of any parameters specified as memory variables in the calling program are passed back to the calling program.

DO CASE . . . ENDCASE

This program structure selects one out of a number of possibilities. The general form of this structure is:

```
DO CASE
   CASE <condition 1>
      <program statements>
   [CASE <condition 2>
      <program statements>]
   [CASE <condition 3>
      <program statements>]
   [<more cases>]
   [OTHERWISE
      <program statements>]
ENDCASE
```

Any number of statements may be included in a CASE. dBASE III PLUS assumes that only one of the CASE statements is true; if more than one is true, only the statements following the first will be executed. If the optional OTHERWISE clause is included, it must follow all of the other CASEs; the statements following OTHERWISE are executed if none of the conditions in the preceding CASE statements is true. If none of the conditions is true and no OTHERWISE clause is included, no action is taken.

DO WHILE . . . ENDDO

This program structure repeats execution of a group of program statements as long as a specified condition remains true. The general form of this structure is:

```
DO WHILE <condition>
   <program statements>
ENDDO
```

If the *condition* is never true, the statements within the loop are not executed even once; if the condition never becomes false, the loop will run forever. dBASE III PLUS checks the condition only once on each pass through the loop, so if the condition becomes false midway through, the remaining statements are still executed unless you exit the loop with EXIT or return to the DO WHILE statement with LOOP to force dBASE III PLUS to reevaluate the condition immediately. If the *condition* contains a macro, it is evaluated only once, on the first pass through the loop, so you cannot use a macro if the value of the variable expanded as a macro is changed within the loop.

EDIT [<*scope*>] [FIELDS <*field list*>] [FOR <*condition*>] [WHILE <*condition*>]

Enters a full-screen mode to edit the specified fields in the range of records defined by the *scope* and *conditions*. If no *scope* is specified, ALL is assumed. EDIT is identical to CHANGE.

EJECT

Ejects the paper in the printer to the top of the next page.

ERASE <*file name*>

Erases the specified file from the disk. Any disk file may be ERASEd with this command, so the extension (and path, if the file is not in the current subdirectory) must be included. Only one file at a time may be ERASEd, and you may not ERASE any file that is currently open.

▪ EXIT

Causes dBASE III PLUS to EXIT immediately from the currently running DO WHILE loop and resume execution with the first command following the ENDDO statement.

EXPORT TO *<file name>* TYPE PFS

Exports data to a PFS file from the data base open in the currently selected work area. If a format file is open, it is used as a model for the PFS screen layout; if not, the PFS screen will resemble the standard dBASE III PLUS data entry screen.

FIND *<character string>/<n>*

Searches the first index named in the USE command that opened the current data base for the specified record. If the index is based on a character string, a literal search string need not be enclosed in quotation marks unless it includes leading blank spaces. When you search for a character string stored in a memory variable, the variable name must be preceded by the macro symbol (&) so that dBASE III PLUS searches for the value of the variable rather than the characters that make up its name. If the index is based on a numeric field, you must specify the key value as a numeric constant, not by storing it in a memory variable. In every other respect, FIND works like SEEK.

GO/GOTO *<expN>*/BOTTOM/TOP

Positions the current data base to the specified record. GOTO BOTTOM positions the data base to the last record in the file or, with an index open, to the last record in indexed order. GOTO TOP positions the data base to the first record in the file or, with an index open, to the first record in indexed order. If you have used SET DELETED ON or SET FILTER to limit the range of records being processed, GOTO TOP or GOTO BOTTOM positions the data base to the first or last record that satisfies all of the specified conditions; however, you may still GOTO any record by number.

HELP [<*keyword*>]

Displays a screen of help text summarizing the syntax and usage of the specified keyword. HELP with no keyword calls up the first screen in the menu-driven help system.

IF . . . ELSE . . . ENDIF

This program structure selects one of two alternatives. The general form of the structure is:

```
IF <condition>
    <program statements>
[ELSE
    <program statements>]
ENDIF
```

If the *condition* is true, the statements following IF (which may include another IF loop) are executed. If the condition is false and the optional ELSE is included, the statements between ELSE and ENDIF are executed. With no ELSE clause, no action is taken.

▶ IMPORT FROM <*file name*> TYPE PFS

Imports data from a PFS file and creates a data base file, a format file that matches the PFS screen layout, and a view file that enables you to open the data base and format file together (with a SET VIEW command).

▶ INDEX ON <*key expression*> TO <*index file name*> [UNIQUE]

Builds an index for the current data base based on the specified *key expression*. If the *key expression* or *file name* is omitted, dBASE III PLUS will prompt you to enter them.The *key expression* may be up to 100 characters long. When the INDEX command completes, dBASE III PLUS leaves the new index open (and closes any other indexes open previously) with the record pointer positioned at the end-of-file.

An index may be based on a single character, numeric, or date field, resulting in alphabetic, ascending numeric, or ascending calendar date order, respectively. If fields of different data types are combined to form the key expression, all must be converted to character strings (using the DTOC function for dates and the STR function for numeric fields).

If the UNIQUE keyword is included, only the first record in a group that shares the same value for the *key expression* is included in the index. Thereafter, whenever the file is opened with this index, it will appear to contain unique index keys.

▪ INPUT [<*expC*>] TO <*memvar*>

Collects input from the user and creates the memory variable *memvar* to store the input. If *expC* is included, it is displayed as a prompt. The data type of the memory variable is determined by the data type of the user's entry, which may be any valid dBASE III PLUS expression. If a syntactically incorrect expression is entered, an error message is displayed and the prompt is repeated. If the user presses RETURN or types only blank spaces, dBASE III PLUS repeats the prompt.

INSERT [BEFORE]

▪ INSERT BLANK

INSERT adds a new record to the current data base, using the standard dBASE III PLUS full-screen edit commands. If BEFORE is included, the new record is placed before the current record; otherwise, it is inserted after the current record. In either case, all of the remaining records are moved down to make room for the new entry, which can be very slow in a large data base. If you have SET CARRY ON, the fields take their default values from the current record, or from the previous record if you have specified the BEFORE option.

An alternative is to use an index to access the file in the desired order and allow new records to be APPENDed to the end of the file. dBASE III PLUS does this automatically if INSERT is used with an index open.

INSERT BLANK adds a blank record to the current data base and positions the record pointer to the new record without invoking the full-screen edit mode. Usually, the fields are filled in with REPLACE or GET commands.

▶ JOIN WITH *<alias>* TO *<file name>* FOR *<condition>* [FIELDS *<field list>*]

Creates a new data base file based on the contents of the current data base and a second file, which is open in another work area and is specified by its *alias*. The two files are matched up record by record, and dBASE III PLUS adds a record to the new data base for each pair of records from the two files that satisfies the *condition*.

If a *field list* is included, it defines the structure of the new file. Otherwise, this file contains all of the fields from the current file plus as many fields from the second as permitted by the 128-field limit, except for memo fields, which are ignored by the JOIN command. No field names will be duplicated even if both files contain fields of the same name. Because dBASE III PLUS reads through the entire second file for each record in the current file, this command can be very time-consuming.

▶ LABEL FORM <*label format file*> [<*scope*>] [FOR <*condition*>] [WHILE <*condition*>] [TO PRINT] [TO FILE <*file name*>] [SAMPLE]

Prints labels from the current data base, using the specified label format file, for the range of records defined by the *scope* and *conditions*. If no *scope* is specified, ALL is assumed. If the label form references fields from more than one data base, all of the necessary data base and index files must be open and the files must be linked with SET RELATION.

TO PRINT causes dBASE III PLUS to print the labels as well as display them on the screen. TO FILE creates a disk file that contains an exact image of the printed labels. SAMPLE causes dBASE III PLUS to print rows of asterisks that occupy the same amount of space as a label to enable you to align the label stock in the printer.

▶ LIST [<*scope*>] [<*exp list*>] [FOR <*condition*>] [WHILE <*condition*>] [TO PRINT] [OFF]

Displays the specified expressions for the range of records in the current data base defined by the *scope* and *conditions*. If no *scope* is specified, ALL is assumed, and with no *exp list*, all fields are included. If you have SET HEADING ON, the listed expressions are displayed as column titles, in the same mixture of uppercase and lowercase used in the LIST command.

The contents of memo fields are displayed only if the field names are explicitly included in the *exp list*. TO PRINT causes dBASE III PLUS to echothe screen display to the printer. OFF suppresses the display of the record numbers. The LIST command is similar to DISPLAY, except that DISPLAY assumes a default *scope* of one record and pauses the display every 20 lines.

LIST FILES [LIKE <*skeleton*>]

This command is identical to DISPLAY FILES, except that the display does not pause when the screen is full, making the LIST version better for printing the listing.

LIST HISTORY [LAST <*expN*>] [TO PRINT]

This command is identical to DISPLAY HISTORY, except that the display does not pause when the screen is full, making the LIST version better for printing the listing.

LIST MEMORY [TO PRINT]

This command is identical to DISPLAY MEMORY, except that the display does not pause when the screen is full, making the LIST version better for printing the listing.

▶ LIST STATUS [TO PRINT]

This command is identical to DISPLAY STATUS, except that the display does not pause when the screen is full, making the LIST version better for printing the listing.

▶ LIST STRUCTURE [TO PRINT]

This command is identical to DISPLAY STRUCTURE, except that the display does not pause when the screen is full, making the LIST version better for printing the listing.

▪ ▶ LOAD <*binary file name*>

Loads a binary file into memory for execution with CALL. Five modules may be LOADed into memory at once. LOAD and CALL should be used only for subroutines written expressly to be executed this way; COM or EXE files (including most commercial software) should be invoked with the RUN command instead.

▶ LOCATE [<*scope*>] [FOR <*condition*>] [WHILE <*condition*>]

Searches the range of records in the current data base defined by the *scope* and WHILE clause for the first record that matches the specified *conditions*. If no *scope* is specified, ALL is assumed. If a matching record is found, the data base is left positioned at this record; if you have SET TALK ON, the record number is displayed. The CONTINUE command may be used to search for additional records that satisfy the same *conditions*. If no matching record is found, an "End of locate scope" message is displayed, and the FOUND() function assumes the value .F.

LOGOUT

In a data base with a PROTECT security system, closes all open files and presents a new log-in screen, exactly as if you had QUIT and reentered dBASE III PLUS.

LOOP

Causes dBASE III PLUS to bypass the remaining steps in a DO WHILE loop and return immediately to the DO WHILE statement to reevaluate the condition.

MODIFY COMMMAND [<*file name*>]
MODIFY FILE [<*file name*>]

Invokes the dBASE III PLUS editor to create or edit a text file, usually a dBASE III PLUS program or format file. If you do not specify the *file name*, dBASE III PLUS will prompt you to enter it. If the file already exists, it is loaded into the editor; if not, a new file is created. The MODIFY COMMAND editor can handle a file up to 5000 characters long. You can use the TEDIT option in CONFIG.DB

(TEDIT = <*program name*>) to substitute another editor or word processor for the dBASE III PLUS editor so that the external program is invoked by MODIFY COMMAND.

MODIFY FILE does not assume that the file to be created or edited is a program file, so you must specify the extension.

▶ MODIFY LABEL <*label file name*>

This command is identical to CREATE LABEL.

▶ MODIFY QUERY <*label file name*>

This command is identical to CREATE QUERY.

▶ MODIFY REPORT <*report file name*>

This command is identical to CREATE REPORT.

▶ MODIFY SCREEN <*label file name*>

This command is identical to CREATE SCREEN.

▶ MODIFY STRUCTURE <*file name*>

Changes the structure of the current data base file and adjusts existing records to match the new structure. dBASE III PLUS creates a temporary copy of the file structure, to which you make your changes;

the data is then appended from the original file and this file is renamed with a BAK (backup) extension.

The same rules that govern the APPEND FROM *<file name>* command apply to transferring data from the backup file to the new structure. You may change field lengths, add or delete fields, or change the data type of a field without losing data (provided that the contents of the field are consistent with the new type). If a character field is shortened, the contents are truncated to fit; numeric data that is too long is replaced with asterisks. If a field is deleted, the data is lost, and, if a field is added, it will be blank in every record. You may change field names, provided that you do not make any other changes at the same time. All indexes must be rebuilt after a file structure is modified.

▶ MODIFY VIEW *<label file name>*

This command is identical to CREATE VIEW.

▪ ▶ NOTE/*

Identifies a statement as a comment (nonexecutable) line in a dBASE III PLUS program. You can also include a comment on the same line as a program statement by preceding the comment with &&.

▪ ▶ ON ERROR/ESCAPE/KEY *<command>*

Specifies a command to be executed under one of three conditions: when an error occurs, when the

ESCAPE key is pressed, or when any key is pressed. The *command* may be any valid dBASE III PLUS command, but it is usually a DO command that invokes another program or procedure, which takes corrective action in response to an error or processes a request to interrupt the currently running program. The three ON commands may be used in any combination; with both ON ESCAPE and ON KEY in effect, pressing ESCAPE activates the ON ESCAPE command rather than the ON KEY command.

ON ESCAPE has no effect if you have disabled the ESC key with SET ESCAPE OFF. An ON KEY procedure will execute correctly only if it includes a command to clear the key pressed by the user from the typeahead buffer. You can do this with the INKEY() function or the READ or CLEAR TYPEAHEAD commands.

PACK

Permanently removes from the current data base all records previously marked for deletion and rebuilds any indexes opened with the data base in the USE command. After a file is PACKed, there is no way to recover the deleted records. PACK reclaims the disk space formerly occupied by the deleted records, but the new file size and number of records are updated on the disk (and therefore reported correctly by the DIR command) only after the file is closed.

▪ ▶ PARAMETERS *<exp list>*

Creates local memory variables corresponding to the values passed to a program or procedure in a DO command. If present, the PARAMETERS command must be the first executable (noncomment) line in the program or procedure. The correspondence between the parameters in the DO command and the PARAMETERS command is established by the order in which they are listed. The parameters may be any valid dBASE III PLUS expressions, but if fields are passed as parameters, the file alias must be specified, even for fields in the currently selected work area. All changes made to the values of any parameters specified as memory variables in the calling program are passed back to the calling program.

▪ ▶ PRIVATE [ALL [LIKE *<skeleton>*]]/ [*<memvar list>*]

Declares the specified memory variables private to the program that created them, so that local variables may be given the same names as PUBLIC variables or variables in a program higher in a chain of programs that call each other.

▪ ▶ PROCEDURE *<procedure name>*

Used to identify the individual procedures in a procedure file. A procedure name may be up to eight characters long. Each procedure must begin with a PROCEDURE command and should end with a RETURN.

▸ PUBLIC <*memvar list*>

Makes the memory variables in the *memvar list* available to all programs in a system. A variable must be declared PUBLIC before it is initialized. Within a program, PUBLIC variables may be erased from memory by naming them explicitly in a RELEASE command or by using CLEAR MEMORY or CLEAR ALL, but not RELEASE ALL.

▸ QUIT

Closes all open disk files and exits from dBASE III PLUS to the operating system.

▸ READ [SAVE]

Allows editing of the variables displayed by all of the @ . . . SAY . . . GET commands issued since the last READ, CLEAR GETs, or CLEAR command. The cursor is positioned initially in the first variable, and the user may edit the data using the standard full-screen cursor movement and editing commands.

If the SAVE option is included, the READ command does not also CLEAR the GETs, so that a subsequent READ may collect the same set of fields again. It is up to you to ensure that you do not allow too many GETs between READ commands. By default, dBASE III PLUS permits 128, but you can increase this to 1023 with an entry in CONFIG.DB.

RECALL [<*scope*>] [FOR <*condition*>] [WHILE <*condition*>]

Recovers ("undeletes") all of the records marked for deletion in the current data base in the range of records defined by the *scope* and *conditions*. If no *scope* is specified, only the current record is RECALLed.

REINDEX

Rebuilds all of the index files opened with the current data base in the USE command, based on the original key expression(s), which are stored in the index file(s). If the original index was created after a SET UNIQUE ON command or if the UNIQUE keyword was specified in the INDEX command, the new index file will also have the UNIQUE attribute. If an index file is damaged, dBASE III PLUS may not be able to read the key expression, and you must use the INDEX command instead.

RELEASE [ALL [LIKE/EXCEPT <*skeleton*>]]/[<*memvar list*>]

RELEASE MODULE

Erases from memory the specified variables and frees the space for defining additional variables. When used in a program, RELEASE ALL erases only variables created within the program.

- **RELEASE MODULE** unloads a binary file placed in memory by the LOAD command.

▶ RENAME *<old file name>* TO *<new file name>*

Renames the specified file. Because you may use this command to rename any disk file, the file extension (or full path name, if the file is not in the current subdirectory) must be specified. If you RENAME a DBF file that contains memo fields, you must also remember to RENAME the corresponding DBT file. Only one file at a time may be renamed, and you may not rename a file that is currently open.

▶ REPLACE [*<scope>*] *<field>* WITH *<exp>* [,*<field2>* WITH *<exp2>* . . .] [FOR *<condition>*] [WHILE *<condition>*]

Substitutes the results of evaluating the listed expressions for the current values of the specified fields, for the range of records in the current data base defined by the *scope* and *conditions*. If no *scope* is specified, only fields in the current record are REPLACEd.

If you REPLACE the values of the key fields in a data base opened with one or more indexes, the indexes are automatically updated. This also means that the index entry for the record is immediately moved to its new location in the index, and the "next" record will not be the same one as before the REPLACE; this type of REPLACEment should therefore not be performed on an indexed file.

▶ REPORT FORM *<report form file>* [*<scope>*] [FOR *<condition>*] [WHILE *<condition>*] [NOEJECT] [PLAIN] [SUMMARY] [HEADING *<expC>*] [TO PRINT] [TO FILE *<file name>*]

Prints a report, using the specified report form file, for the range of records from the current data base defined by the *scope* and *conditions*. If no *scope* is specified, ALL is assumed. If the report form references fields from more than one data base, all of the necessary data base and index files must be open, and the files must be linked with SET RELATION.

TO PRINT causes dBASE III PLUS to print the report as well as display it on the screen. TO FILE creates a disk file that contains an exact image of the printed report. The HEADING clause may be used to specify an optional extra heading line that is printed on the first line of each page, centered above the page title.

The NOEJECT, PLAIN, and SUMMARY keywords may be used to override the values for the corresponding parameters defined in the report form. NOEJECT suppresses the page eject normally sent to the printer before beginning the report. PLAIN causes dBASE III PLUS to print the report with no date or page numbers, and to print the page title and column headings only once, on the first page. SUMMARY produces a report that includes only subtotals, sub-subtotals, and totals, with no detail records.

▶ RESTORE FROM *<file name>* [ADDITIVE]

Loads the variables in the specified memory file into memory. Without the ADDITIVE option, any existing variables are first RELEASEd. If the command was issued from within a program, the newly loaded variables become PRIVATE; if it was typed from the dot prompt, they are PUBLIC. If the ADDITIVE option is included, the variables in the memory file are *added* to the ones currently in memory. With the ADDITIVE option, variables stored as PUBLIC become PUBLIC again, provided that you declare them PUBLIC prior to the RESTORE command.

▶ RESUME

Continues to execute a program previously interrupted with the ESCAPE key and suspended (rather than cancelled). Execution resumes with the command following the one interrupted by the ESCAPE key.

▶ RETRY

Returns control from the currently running program to the calling program. Execution resumes with the command that caused the second program to be called instead of the next one. This command is often used in a network environment to attempt to lock a file or record that might be locked by another user, and in error-handling procedures to allow the user to correct the error condition, after which the program retries the operation that caused the error.

▪ ▶ RETURN [TO MASTER]

Causes dBASE III PLUS to exit from the current program or procedure and return control to the calling program or procedure or to the dot prompt (if the program was invoked from the dot prompt). Execution resumes with the command following the DO command that called the second program. RETURN TO MASTER jumps to the highest level dBASE III PLUS program (the user's first entry point into the system) instead of to the calling program. A RETURN command may occur anywhere within a program. If there is no RETURN command, a program terminates after the last statement is executed.

▶ RUN *<command>*

! *<command>*

Executes the specified MS-DOS command, batch file, or program. COMMAND.COM must be available, either in the root directory of the disk from which the system was booted or, under DOS 3, in any subdirectory identified to DOS with a SET COMSPEC command. You must have enough additional memory in your computer beyond the 256K required for running dBASE III PLUS to load COMMAND.COM and the external program into RAM along with dBASE III PLUS.

▶ SAVE TO <*file name*> [ALL LIKE/EXCEPT <*skeleton*>]

Saves the specified memory variables on disk in the named memory variable file. If it includes an ALL LIKE or ALL EXCEPT clause, only memory variables with names that match the skeleton are SAVEd.

▶ SEEK <*exp*>

Searches the index named first in the USE command that opened the current data base for data matching the specified expression. You may search on less than the full index key value, but the portion you specify must begin at the start of the field. SEEK is similar to FIND, except that FIND can accept only a single numeric or character string constant as its object, whereas SEEK can accept any valid expression.

If the search succeeds, the data base is positioned at the first record in which the index key matches the value of the *expression*. The FOUND() function has the value .T., and EOF() is .F. If there is no matching record, dBASE III PLUS displays the message "No Find", positions the data base at the end-of-file, and sets the EOF() function to .T. and FOUND() to .F.

▶ SELECT <*work area/alias*>

Switches to the specified work area. A work area may always be selected by number (1 to 10) or by letter (A to J), and any work area in which a data base is open may also be selected by the file's alias.

When you SELECT a work area, any data bases open in other work areas remain positioned exactly where they were. Fields from these files may be specified for display or for use in calculations using the notation *alias->field name*.

SET

Invokes a menu-driven, full-screen mode for viewing and changing many of the SET options. The options are described individually. Note that the default values of options with two or more alternate values are indicated in uppercase.

SET ALTERNATE TO [*<file name>*]
SET ALTERNATE on/OFF

SET ALTERNATE TO *<file name>* opens the specified text file. Once the file is open, SET ALTERNATE ON causes dBASE III PLUS to echo all sequential screen output (all text except that displayed by the full-screen commands) to the text file. SET ALTERNATE OFF suspends recording in the ALTERNATE file. You may SET ALTERNATE ON and OFF as many times as necessary during a work session. To close the text file, use CLOSE ALTERNATE or SET ALTERNATE TO after the last SET ALTERNATE OFF command.

▶ SET BELL ON/off

Determines whether or not dBASE III PLUS sounds the computer's bell (usually a beeper) when the user's entry completely fills a field or when a data entry error is made (for example, typing an invalid date or entering characters into a numeric field).

▶ SET CARRY on/OFF

Determines whether or not the data entered into each new record APPENDed to a data base serves as the default field values for the next record entered. The status of the CARRY option affects only records added with the full-screen APPEND or INSERT commands; even if you SET CARRY ON, all of the fields in a record added with APPEND BLANK or INSERT BLANK remain blank.

▶ SET CATALOG TO [<*catalog file name*>]

SET CATALOG on/OFF

SET CATALOG TO <*catalog file name*> opens the specified catalog data base in work area 10 or creates it if it does not exist. A CATALOG is a normal dBASE III PLUS data base file with the extension CAT instead of DBF, which may be displayed and updated from the dot prompt as long as you do not change the structure.

The CATALOG records all files used in an application and their associations. With a CATALOG open, the file lists displayed by the ASSIST menus include only files in the CATALOG, and a CATALOG query clause — substituting a "?" where dBASE III PLUS expects a file name — may be used in any command issued from the dot prompt to call up a list of available files of the correct type and, where appropriate, associated with the specified data base.

When a CATALOG is open, it is updated when files are created, renamed, or deleted. When a new file is added to the CATALOG, if you have SET TITLE ON, dBASE III PLUS will prompt you to enter an 80-character title, which is then displayed along with the file name in response to a CATALOG query clause. You can temporarily disable the CATALOG update process with SET CATALOG OFF and reactivate it with SET CATALOG ON.

SET CENTURY on/OFF

Determines whether dates are displayed and entered with four-digit years. With CENTURY OFF, the century is assumed to be 1900 and the year is always displayed as two digits; nevertheless, if a calculation creates a value for a date field in another century, the century is stored and used in subsequent calculations. With CENTURY ON, all dates are displayed and entered with four-digit years.

► SET COLOR TO [<*standard foreground/standard background*>] [,<*enhanced foreground/enhanced background*>] [, <*border*>]

SET COLOR on/off

SET COLOR TO determines the colors or monochrome display attributes used for information displayed by dBASE III PLUS (the *standard* display), data entered by the user (the *enhanced* display), and the *border* (the area of the screen outside the 24-line by 80-column display area). If any of the five values are omitted, the defaults are used: white letters on a black background for the standard area, black letters on a white background for the enhanced area, and black for the border.

SET COLOR ON/OFF selects between color and monochrome displays if both are present. The default value matches the monitor in use when dBASE III PLUS was loaded.

► SET CONFIRM on/OFF

Determines whether the operator must confirm each field or memory variable entry by pressing RETURN. If you SET CONFIRM ON, the cursor does not advance automatically to the next item when the data entry area is filled completely — the user must press RETURN.

▪ ▶ SET CONSOLE ON/off

Determines whether sequential output appears on the console (the screen). Data displayed in the full-screen edit modes is not affected by the status of this setting. SET CONSOLE OFF may be used to prevent data printed by REPORT, LABEL, or ? commands from also appearing on the screen. Even if you SET CONSOLE OFF, input may be entered by the operator, although it is not echoed to the screen, and all dBASE III PLUS error messages are displayed.

▶ SET DATE AMERICAN/ansi/british/ italian/french/german

Establishes the display format for date fields and memory variables. No matter which display format is in effect, dBASE III PLUS can carry out date arithmetic and date comparisons, and it can SORT or INDEX on a single date field in correct chronological order. These are the formats:

AMERICAN	MM/DD/YY
ANSI	YY.MM.DD
BRITISH	DD/MM/YY
ITALIAN	DD-MM-YY
FRENCH	DD.MM.YY
GERMAN	DD.MM.YY

▪ ▶ SET DEBUG on/OFF

Determines whether the command lines echoed by SET ECHO ON are displayed on the screen or printed on the printer. If you SET DEBUG ON, the output of the ECHO option is routed to the printer so that formatted screens are not disrupted by the echoed program lines.

▶ SET DECIMALS TO <*expN*>

Determines the number of decimal places displayed when an expression involving division or the SQRT, LOG, or EXP function is evaluated. The default is 2, and you may specify any value between 0 and 15. If you also SET FIXED ON, the SET DECIMALS option controls the display of all numeric variables and calculations, not just those involving division, SQRT, LOG, or EXP. In calculations involving multiplication, the number of decimal places in the result is equal to the sum of the number of decimal places in the two quantities multiplied. Otherwise, it is the same as in the quantity with the most decimal places.

▶ SET DEFAULT TO <*drive*>

Establishes the default disk drive to be used by dBASE III PLUS to read and write all disk files unless a different drive is explicitly included with the file name.

SET DELETED on/OFF

Determines whether dBASE III PLUS processes records that have been marked for deletion. If you SET DELETED ON, deleted records are ignored in all commands, except when the record number is specified explicitly (for example, in an explicit GOTO command or a command with a *scope* of a single record). If SET DELETED ON is issued with a file already open, it does not automatically reposition the record pointer to the first nondeleted record; you can use GOTO TOP for this purpose.

SET DELIMITERS TO [<*delimiter(s)*>] [DEFAULT]

SET DELIMITERS on/OFF

SET DELIMITERS ON/OFF determines whether fields displayed by GET commands are surrounded by delimiters. SET DELIMITERS TO <*delimiters*> designates the actual delimiter character(s). You may specify either one or two characters, enclosed in quotes. If you specify one character, it is used as both the beginning and ending delimiter; if you specify two, the first is used as the beginning delimiter and the second as the ending delimiter. If you SET DELIMITERS ON without assigning delimiters, a colon (:) is used. The DEFAULT option restores this default delimiter after a previous SET DELIMITERS TO command.

▪ ► SET DEVICE TO printer/SCREEN

Determines whether the output of @ . . . SAY commands is routed to the printer or to the screen. When you have SET DEVICE TO PRINT, all GET clauses are ignored.

▪ ► SET DOHISTORY on/OFF

Determines whether commands executed from dBASE III PLUS programs are recorded in the history list, along with the commands you type from the dot prompt. This option is most often used as a debugging aid, to enable you to retrace execution of a program after a test run. If you SET DOHISTORY ON, you will usually want to increase the number of commands retained in history (from the default 20) with SET HISTORY TO.

▪ ► SET ECHO on/OFF

Determines whether command lines are echoed to the screen as they are executed. All commands are echoed, including those typed at the dot prompt, but this option is most frequently used to monitor the progress of a program or to trace execution for debugging purposes. If you also SET DEBUG ON, the echoed command lines are routed to the printer instead of to the console so that formatted screen displays are not disrupted.

▶ SET ENCRYPTION ON/off

In a data base with a PROTECT security system in effect, determines whether new files created by copying existing data bases (with commands such as COPY or SORT) are encrypted. The status of this option does not affect files defined with the CREATE command; these must be encrypted through the PROTECT program. ENCRYPTION must be OFF in order to COPY or EXPORT a data base file to one of the external formats supported by dBASE III PLUS — DELIMITED, SDF, DIF, SYLK, WKS, and PFS.

▪ ▶ SET ESCAPE ON/off

Determines whether dBASE III PLUS responds when the user presses the ESC key. If you SET ESCAPE OFF, a dBASE III PLUS command or program can be interrupted only by rebooting or turning off the computer.

▶ SET EXACT on/OFF

Determines whether character strings are compared using the full length of both strings. If you SET EXACT OFF, dBASE III PLUS examines only the number of characters in the string on the right side of the equals sign, if this string is shorter. If you SET EXACT ON, the two strings are considered equal only if they are the same length and have the same value.

▶ SET EXCLUSIVE ON/off

In a network environment, determines whether files are opened in exclusive or shared mode. The file open mode is determined by the status of the EXCLUSIVE option at the time a file is opened, even if you subsequently reset the EXCLUSIVE option. Any file opened with EXCLUSIVE OFF can only be accessed by one user at a time. If a file is opened in shared mode, a file or record locking system should be implemented to prevent damage caused by multiple simultaneous updates. A file may also be opened for exclusive use by including the EXCLUSIVE keyword in the USE command.

▶ SET FIELDS TO [<*field list*>/ALL] SET FIELDS on/OFF

SET FIELDS TO <*field list*> specifies the fields from one or more open data bases that are accessible to most dBASE III PLUS commands. SET FIELDS ON activates the field list defined with SET FIELDS commands, and SET FIELDS OFF temporarily disables the field list. Regardless of the order in which the fields are named in the SET FIELDS command, they are presented in the full-screen edit modes in the order they occur in the file structure(s).

Successive SET FIELDS commands add to the field list, so you are not limited by the 254-character command length limit. However, the ALL option sets the field list to all fields in the current data base, and no others. To access all fields from the current data base, together with selected fields from other work areas, the SET FIELDS TO ALL command must therefore precede the other SET FIELDS commands.

To access fields from more than one file in a meaningful way, the files must share a common key, and they must be linked with SET RELATION; usually this means that, for each record in the selected data base, there is only one matching record in the file accessed through the RELATION. When the related file is selected, no fields in other data bases are displayed by commands, such as EDIT and DISPLAY.

Even with a field list in effect, APPEND and INSERT add records only to the file in the currently selected work area, and display all the fields in the structure. INDEX, LOCATE, SET FILTER, and SET RELATION commands may access any fields in all work areas. All fields remain accessible in open files that are not named in a SET FIELDS command or related to a file affected by the field list.

► SET FILTER TO [<*condition*>]/[FILE <*query file name*>]

Establishes a condition that determines which records are processed by all dBASE III PLUS commands. With a FILTER in effect, records that do not pass the condition in the filter are ignored, except when the record number is specified explicitly (for example, in an explicit GOTO command or with a *scope* of a single record). SET FILTER TO FILE reads a condition previously stored in a query file constructed with CREATE QUERY.

All commands that position the data base act relative to the FILTER, but the SET FILTER command itself does not reposition the record pointer, even if the current record does not pass the FILTER *condition*; you can use GOTO TOP for this purpose. A separate FILTER may be in effect in each active work area, but, with any work area selected, only the FILTER in this area is recognized by dBASE III PLUS. A FILTER may also reference fields in data bases open in other work areas, but this usually makes sense only if the files are linked with SET RELATION.

SET FILTER TO, with no *condition*, cancels the FILTER in the current work area. If a FILTER depends on fields in more than one file, you must be sure to cancel the FILTER if any of the files involved are closed.

SET FIXED on/OFF

Determines whether dBASE III PLUS displays all numeric expressions with a fixed number of decimal places. If you SET FIXED ON, the SET DECIMALS option determines the number of decimals displayed for all numeric variables; otherwise, SET DECIMALS affects only the results of calculations involving division, SQRT, LOG, or EXP.

SET FORMAT TO [<*format file name*>]

Opens a format file that draws a formatted data entry screen for the full-screen APPEND, EDIT, CHANGE, and INSERT commands. SET FORMAT TO, with no file name, or CLOSE FORMAT closes the format file open in the current work area.

SET FUNCTION <*exp*> TO <*expC*>

Assigns a new meaning to one of the programmable function keys. On most IBM and compatible computers, there are 10 or 12 function keys, referred to by the numbers 2 through 10 or 12 (or numeric expressions that evaluate to these values). You may not assign a new value to the HELP key (usually F1), which is reserved for invoking the dBASE III PLUS menu-driven help system. Each of the other function keys may be assigned any arbitrary sequence of characters. In this string, pressing ENTER may be symbolized by a semicolon (;).

SET HEADING ON/off

Determines whether dBASE III PLUS displays column headings in LIST, DISPLAY, SUM, COUNT, and AVERAGE commands. If you SET HEADING ON, the field names, variable names, or expressions are displayed as column headings, in the same mixture of uppercase and lowercase used in the command. The width of each column of data on the screen is the width of the quantity displayed or the column heading, whichever is greater.

▶ SET HELP ON/off

Determines whether dBASE III PLUS displays the message "Do you want some help? (Y/N)" when a syntax error is made in a command typed at the dot prompt.

▶ SET HISTORY TO <*expN*>
SET HISTORY ON/off

SET HISTORY determines the number of commands that are retained in the history list. The default is 20, and you may specify any value between 0 and 16,000. SET HISTORY OFF temporarily disables the history feature, and SET HISTORY ON turns it back on.

▶ SET INDEX TO [<*index file list*>]

Opens the specified index file(s) together with the current data base. You may open up to seven indexes for each data base, all of which are updated to reflect new entries and changes made to the key fields. The index named first in the *index file list* is the *master index*, which determines the order in which records are displayed or printed; this is the only index that may be used to retrieve records with FIND or SEEK. The SET INDEX command positions the data base to the record that matches the first index entry. SET INDEX TO, with no list of index files, or CLOSE INDEX closes all indexes in the current work area.

SET INTENSITY ON/off

Determines whether the *standard* display colors or monochrome attributes used for data displayed by dBASE III PLUS are the same as the *enhanced* display colors used for data entered by the user. SET INTENSITY OFF eliminates the difference between these two areas and uses the same colors for the *enhanced* that were SET for the *standard* area.

SET MARGIN TO <*expN*>

Establishes the left margin used for all printed output, including reports and the output of LIST TO PRINT and DISPLAY TO PRINT commands. The default is 0. For reports and labels, this value is added to the margin specified in the report or label form.

SET MEMOWIDTH TO <*expN*>

Determines the display width for memo fields in LIST, DISPLAY, and ? commands.The default is 50.

SET MENUS on/OFF

Determines whether a help menu listing the cursor movement and editing commands is displayed by default in the full-screen edit modes. Regardless of the status of this setting, you may always toggle the menu on or off by pressing F1.

▶ SET MESSAGE TO [<*expC*>]

Defines a character string up to 79 characters long that is displayed on line 24 of the screen. The message is only displayed if you have also SET STATUS ON, but it is replaced by the standard dBASE III PLUS messages in menu-driven commands, such as ASSIST or any of the full-screen CREATE/MODIFY editors.

▶ SET ODOMETER TO [<*expN*>]

Determines how frequently dBASE III PLUS updates the display of the number of records processed by such commands as APPEND, COPY, and COUNT. The display is updated every *expN* records; higher values for ODOMETER will result in slightly faster command execution. The default is 1.

▶ SET ORDER TO [<*expN*>]

Determines which of the indexes opened with the data base in the current work area is the master index (the one that controls the order in which records are processed and the one used for FIND and SEEK commands). The *expN* evaluates to a number that corresponds to the position of the index in the index file list in the USE command that opened the data base. SET INDEX TO 0 causes dBASE III PLUS to process the file in sequential order, as if no indexes were open. SET ORDER is a faster way to switch indexes than SET INDEX, because no files are actually opened or closed.

SET PATH TO [<*path name list*>]

Establishes the search path used by dBASE III PLUS to find disk files not present in the current subdirectory. APPEND FROM, the CREATE/MODIFY editors, DO, LABEL, REPORT, RESTORE, SET PROCEDURE, TYPE, and USE all use the search path. The COPY, CREATE, INDEX, JOIN, SAVE, and SORT commands, which also create files, search the specified path for files of the same name if you have SET SAFETY ON. However, all new files created by any dBASE III PLUS commands are written in the current subdirectory if you do not specify a full path name.

Regardless of the PATH, DIR (with no path name included), DELETE FILE, ERASE, RENAME, and SET ALTERNATE TO act only on files in the current subdirectory unless a full path name is specified. SET PATH TO behaves much like the MS-DOS PATH command. It does *not* have the same effect as the MS-DOS CHDIR (change directory) command (the way SET DEFAULT TO <*drive*> is equivalent to switching the currently logged disk drive). SET PATH TO, with no path names listed, cancels any previously established search path.

SET PRINT on/OFF

Determines whether sequential output (all text except that displayed by the full-screen commands) sent to the console is also echoed to the printer.

SET PRINTER TO [<*DOS device name*>] [\\SPOOLER/<*computer name*>\ <*printer name*>=<*DOS device name*>]

SET PRINTER TO <*DOS device name*> selects the local printer, specified by the DOS name of the output port (for example, LPT1: or COM1:), to be used for printed output. The default is LPT1:. This command is equivalent to the MS-DOS MODE command for redirecting printer output, which may be used instead, either before you load dBASE III PLUS or with a RUN command. If output is redirected to a serial printer, the baud rate and other communications parameters must first be set with a MODE command.

In a network environment, SET PRINTER TO *computer name**printer name=DOS device name* routes output to a network printer via the network print spooler. This printer is identified by the network computer and printer names in an IBM network, or as SPOOLER in a Novell network.

SET PRINTER TO redirects printed output to the default printer assigned at the operating system level.In a network environment, it also empties the print spooling file.

SET PROCEDURE TO [<*procedure file name*>]

Opens the specified procedure file, which may contain up to 32 separate procedures. SET PROCEDURE TO, with no procedure file name listed, or CLOSE PROCEDURE closes the current procedure file.

▶ SET RELATION TO [<*key expression*> /RECNO()/<*expN*> INTO <*alias*>]

Establishes a relationship between the currently open data base and a data base open in another work area, which is specified by its alias. Only one RELATION may be SET from any given work area, but multiple RELATIONS may be SET into the same work area from two or more other data bases. The files may be linked by record number or based on a common field or fields.

To link the files by record number, you must open the second file with no index. If the RECNO() option is included, or no TO clause is specified, the files are linked so that the record pointer in the second file is always positioned to the same record number as the first file. If a numeric expression is specified in a TO clause, moving the record pointer in the first file automatically positions the second file to the record number specified by *expN*.

To link two files by a common key, the *key expression* must be present in both files (although the component fields need not have the same names), and the second file must be indexed by this expression. With the RELATION in effect, moving the record pointer in the first file automatically positions the second file to the record with the matching value of the key expression, exactly as if you had executed a FIND or SEEK command.

In either case, if dBASE III PLUS fails to find a matching record, the second file is positioned at the end-of-file, the EOF() function is .T., and FOUND() is .F. in the second work area. SET RELATION

TO, with no RELATION specified, cancels the RELATION SET from the current work area.

SET SAFETY ON/off

Determines whether dBASE III PLUS displays a warning message and requests confirmation before executing any command (such as COPY, INDEX, or SORT) that would overwrite an existing disk file.

SET SCOREBOARD ON/off

Determines whether or not dBASE III PLUS displays status indicators (such as *Del* and *Ins*) and error messages (for example, when an invalid date is entered) on the top line of the screen.If you have SET STATUS ON, these messages are displayed in the *status bar*, and error messages appear on line 24; with STATUS OFF, all the scoreboard information is displayed on line 0. If you SET STATUS OFF and also SET SCOREBOARD OFF, the error messages are not displayed, but dBASE III PLUS still refuses to allow the cursor to advance beyond a field that contains invalid data until the entry is corrected.

SET STATUS ON/off

Determines whether dBASE III PLUS uses the last three lines on the screen for a status display. The *status bar* on line 22 displays the current disk drive, data base if one is open, current record or command, whether the current record is deleted, and the status of the INS, NUMLOCK, and CAPSLOCK keys. In a network environment, the *status bar* also informs you whether the current file was opened for exclusive or Read-Only use and whether the current file or record is locked. Line 23 is used for a *navigation line* that describes how to choose among available command options, and line 24 contains a message (which you may customize with SET MESSAGE) describing your options. Even if you have SET STATUS OFF, the status display is always present in menu-driven commands, such as ASSIST and the CREATE/MODIFY editors. A format file designed for use with STATUS ON should not display data on lines 22 through 24.

▪ ▶ SET STEP on/OFF

Determines whether dBASE III PLUS runs programs in single-step mode. If you SET STEP ON, dBASE III PLUS pauses after executing each program line. Pressing ESC cancels the program, S suspends execution, and pressing the space bar causes dBASE III PLUS to execute the next command. SET STEP ON is usually used, together with SET TALK ON and SET ECHO ON (which displays each command line as it is executed), to debug dBASE III PLUS programs.

▶ SET TALK ON/off

Determines whether dBASE III PLUS displays the results of the actions taken in response to your commands — for example, the values STOREd to memory variables, the record number of the new current record after a SKIP or LOCATE command, and the status messages that monitor the progress of commands that process entire data bases (such as INDEX, DELETE, COPY, COUNT, and REPLACE).

SET TITLE ON/off

Determines whether dBASE III PLUS prompts you for a title, or description, for each new file created when a CATALOG is open. If you SET TITLE OFF, files are still added to the CATALOG, but the TITLE field is left blank.

SET TYPEAHEAD TO <*expN*>

Specifies the size of the typeahead buffer. The default is 20, and you may specify any value between 0 (which disables the typeahead buffer) and 32,000. The buffer is also disabled if you SET ESCAPE OFF. If you SET TYPEAHEAD TO 0, commands and functions that depend on the typeahead buffer (ON KEY and INKEY()) will no longer work.

SET UNIQUE on/OFF

Determines whether an index can contain duplicate key entries.If you SET UNIQUE ON and then build an index, it will contain only one entry for any given key value. This option may be used to determine if the data base itself contains any duplicate key values (by checking to see if the number of records indexed equals the number of records in the file) or to prepare a list of all of the possible key values (by COPYing all or some of the fields with the index open). Since such an index may not contain pointers to all of the records, it should *not* be used to access the data base for adding new records or editing existing data.

▶ SET VIEW TO <*view file name*>

Opens all the files specified in the <*view file*>, including data bases, indexes, and the optional format file if one is included in the view, and selects the work area specified when the view was defined. If the view includes RELATIONs, a FILTER condition, or a field list, these are also placed in effect.

▶ SKIP [<*expN*>]

Moves the record pointer forward (if *expN* is positive) or backward (if *expN* is negative) the specified number of records; a SKIP command with no *expN* moves the pointer forward one record. If an index is open, dBASE III PLUS moves forward or backward in the index *expN* entries and then repositions the record pointer to the corresponding record. If you have SET DELETED ON or if you have SET a FILTER, only records that satisfy all the selection criteria are counted.

If you SKIP past the last record in a file, the data base is positioned at a blank record (which is *not* actually added to the file), and the EOF() function is set to .T. If you SKIP backward past the first record in the file, the record pointer remains positioned at the first record in the file and the BOF() function is set to .T.

SORT TO *<new file name>* ON *<field1>* [/A]/[/D] [/C] [, *<field2>* [/A]/[/D] . . .] [*<scope>*] [FOR *<condition>*] [WHILE *<condition>*]

Creates a new data base file containing the range of records from the current data base defined by the *scope* and *conditions*. You may SORT on up to ten fields. The first field determines the major sort order, within which records are sorted according to the second field, and so on.

The sort order may be qualified by three optional parameters: /A (or the keyword ASCENDING) specifies ascending (low to high) order (the default); /D (or DESCENDING) specifies descending (high to low) order; and /C specifies *case-independence*, which treats uppercase and lowercase versions of a letter as equivalent. (Normally, the sort order parallels the sequence of the ASCII character codes, and all of the uppercase letters precede all of the lowercase letters.) If you combine the A or D options with the C option, only one slash is required, for example, /AC.

You may SORT on any combination of numeric, character, and date fields (not logical or memo fields), but the sort keys must be whole fields. To create a file sorted on a more complex expression, you can build an index based on the desired expression and then COPY the file with the index open.

▶ STORE *<exp>* to *<memvar list>* *<memvar>=<exp>*

STORE creates the named variables and assigns them the initial values and data types specified by the *expression.* Using the equals sign syntax, only one memory variable at a time may be created.

▶ SUM [*<scope>*] [*<expN list>*] [FOR*<condition>*] [WHILE *<condition>*] [TO*<memvar list>*]

Calculates the sum for each expression in the list for the range of records defined by the *scope* and *conditions.* If no expressions are listed, all numeric fields in the current data base are SUMmed. If no scope is specified, ALL is assumed. If you have SET TALK ON, the sums are displayed on the screen, and if you have SET HEADING ON, the listed expressions are displayed above the results. If a list of memory variables is included, the named numeric variables are created to store the sums.

▪ ▶ SUSPEND

Temporarily suspends execution of a program and returns control to the dot prompt without closing any files or RELEASEing memory variables. This is equivalent to choosing the Suspend option after pressing ESCAPE to interrupt the currently running program. SUSPEND is used primarily for debugging purposes, to pause a program at a specific point. While the program is suspended, you can type any commands at the dot prompt and then use the RESUME command to continue from the point of interruption or the CANCEL command to cancel the program and return to the dot prompt.

▶ TEXT . . . ENDTEXT

A program structure used to display or print a block of text. The text between TEXT and ENDTEXT is displayed (if you have SET CONSOLE ON) or printed (if you have SET PRINT ON) without processing or interpretation by dBASE III PLUS.

▶ TOTAL ON <*key field*> TO <*file name*> [<*scope*>] [FIELDS <*field list*>] [FOR <*condition*>] [WHILE <*condition*>]

Creates a new data base containing summarized data for the specified numeric fields in the current data base for the range of records defined by the *scope* and *conditions*. If no *field list* is included, all numeric fields are TOTALed. The new file has the same structure as the current data base, except that memo fields are not included. Each record in the new file contains totals for a group of records in the current file with the same value in the *key field*. The current file must be either sorted or indexed on the *key field*, and the numeric fields must be large enough to accommodate the totals.

▶ TYPE *<file name>* [TO PRINT]

Displays the contents of the specified file on the screen. TO PRINT causes dBASE III PLUS to print the file as well as displaying it on the screen.

▪ ▶ UNLOCK [ALL]

In a network environment, releases the most recent lock placed on the file in the currently selected work area. This may be a file lock placed in effect by a call to the FLOCK() function, or a record lock effected by a call to the LOCK() or RLOCK() function. If the ALL keyword is included, all locks in all work areas are released.

▶ UPDATE ON *<key field>* FROM *<alias>* REPLACE *<field1>* WITH *<exp1>* [,*<field2>* WITH *<exp2>* . . .] [RANDOM]

Updates the current data base based on information contained in a second file, which is open in another work area and is specified by its *alias*. Records are matched up based on the content of the *key field*, which must be present in both files. The current file must be either sorted or indexed on the common key field. If the second file is not also sorted or indexed on this field, the RANDOM keyword must be included in the command, and the current file must be indexed, *not* sorted on the common key (this is the most efficient way to use the UPDATE command), so that dBASE III PLUS may use an internal SEEK to find the right record to UPDATE. For each record in the second file, the designated fields in the matching record in the current file are replaced with the specified expressions, which may reference any fields from both files.

▶ USE [<*file name*>] [INDEX <*index file list*>] [ALIAS <*alias*>] [EXCLUSIVE]

Opens the specified data base in the currently selected work area, together with up to seven indexes. If you do not specify an alias, dBASE III PLUS automatically assigns the file name as the alias. If an alias is specified, it must be used in place of the file name in the standard *alias->field name* notation for referring to fields in work areas other than the currently selected area.

If no indexes are listed, the USE command leaves the data base positioned at the first record. If one or more indexes are opened with the file, the data base is positioned to the record corresponding to the first entry in the first index named (the master index).

In a network environment, if the keyword EXCLUSIVE is included, the file is opened for exclusive rather than shared use, and only one workstation at a time may access the file. This is equivalent to issuing a SET EXCLUSIVE ON command prior to opening the file. A file must be opened for exclusive use in order to use commands that affect the entire data base, including INSERT, MODIFY STRUCTURE, PACK, REINDEX, and ZAP.

USE, with no file name, closes the data base and all associated index and format files in the current work area.

▶ WAIT [<*expC*>] [TO <*memvar*>]

Pauses execution of the current program until a key is pressed. If *expC* is included, it is displayed as a prompt; otherwise, dBASE III PLUS displays its default prompt, "Press any key to continue. . .". If a TO clause is included, a character memory variable with the specified name is created to store the operator's keystroke. If the operator presses ENTER, *memvar* will become a null string of length zero.

▶ ZAP

Empties the current data base of all records. This command is equivalent to DELETE ALL, followed by PACK. ZAP operates much faster because it does not actually process all of the records, but instead moves the end-of-file marker and resets the record count to 0. Any indexes opened with the data base in the USE command are adjusted to match the new empty file.

FUNCTIONS

All dBASE III PLUS functions are expressed as the name of the function followed by the function's input(s) (also referred to as "arguments") in parentheses. Even if the function requires no explicit input, parentheses are used to distinguish the function from a field or memory variable with the same name. A function is considered to have the data type of the output it produces, and it may be used anywhere that an expression of that type is permitted. Functions that are used primarily in dBASE III PLUS programs are marked with a square (▪).

▶ &(<*character variable*>)

Substitutes the *value* of the named variable for the variable name. The macro can be used to provide variable input in contexts in which dBASE III PLUS expects a field name, condition, or command. A macro *must* be used in certain commands, like FIND, in which dBASE III PLUS automatically interprets the following word literally, to cause dBASE III PLUS to use the *content* of the variable, not the name.

▶ ABS(<*number*>)

Input: Numeric expression
Output: Number

Evaluates to the absolute value of the numeric expression. The absolute value of a negative number is the positive number with the same magnitude; the absolute value of a positive number is identical to the number itself.

▶ ACCESS()

Input: None
Output: Number

Evaluates to the access level of the last user to log into a multiuser system or to 0 in a single-user system. This function may be used to control access to a menu option or to allow a single option to call two or more different programs, depending on which user requests the option.

▶ ASC(<*character string*>)

Input: Character string expression
Output: Number

Evaluates to the decimal ASCII code of the first character in the character string expression.

▶ AT(<*character string 1*>, <*character string 2*>)

Input: Character string expression, character string expression
Output: Number

Evaluates to the starting position of character string 1 in character string 2 or to 0 if the first string is not found anywhere within the second.

▶ BOF()

Input: None
Output: Logical value

Evaluates to .T. when you attempt to move the record pointer backward past the beginning-of-file by executing a SKIP *-n* command. If the data base is opened without any indexes, the beginning-of-file is the first record. With an index open, it is the record corresponding to the first index entry. After the SKIP *-n* command, the data base remains positioned at the first record.

▶ CDOW(<*expD*>)

Input: Date expression
Output: Character string

Evaluates to a character string containing the name of the day of the week corresponding to the specified date.

▶ CHR(<*number*>)

Input: Numeric expression
Output: Character

Evaluates to a character string consisting of the single character specified by the decimal ASCII code represented by the numeric expression.

▶ CMONTH(<*date*>)

Input: Date expression
Output: Character string

Evaluates to a character string containing the name of the month corresponding to the specified date.

▶ COL()

Input: None
Output: Number

Evaluates to a number representing the current cursor column (horizontal) position on the screen. This function may be used to display data immediately following the last item displayed or a fixed number of columns away from the last item, without reference to the absolute cursor position.

▶ CTOD(<*character expression*>)

Input: Character expression
Output: Date

Evaluates to a true date matching the character string representation of the date supplied as input. Using this function is the only way to express a constant date in dBASE III PLUS, and it must be used anywhere a constant date is required, for example, to initialize a date memory variable, REPLACE a date field with a constant value, or compare a date variable with a constant date.

DATE()

Input: None
Output: Date

The system date as obtained from the operating system.

DAY(<*date*>)

Input: Date expression
Output: Number

Evaluates to a number representing the day of the month in the specified date.

DBF()

Input: None
Output: Character string

Evaluates to a character string consisting of the full name (or path name, if the file is not in the current subdirectory) of the data base open in the current work area or a null string if no data base is open.

DELETED()

Input: None
Output: Logical value

Evaluates to .T. if the current record is marked for deletion or .F. if it is not.

DISKSPACE()

Input: None
Output: Number

Evaluates to the number of bytes of free space remaining on the disk in the currently logged drive. This function may be used to test whether enough space remains before beginning a SORT or COPY command. To determine the disk space remaining on a drive other than the current drive, you may reset the default drive with the SET DEFAULT command.

DOW(<*date*>)

Input: Date expression
Output: Number

Evaluates to a number representing the day of the week in the specified date.

DTOC (<*date*>)

Input: Date expression
Output: Character string

Evaluates to a character string representation of the date expression supplied as input. This function is often used to convert a date to a character string so that it may be concatenated with another character string for display or printing, or for use in an index key expression.

EOF()

Input: None
Output: Logical value

Evaluates to .T. when you attempt to move the record pointer past the end-of-file by executing a SKIP *n* command. If the data base is open without any indexes, the end-of-file is the last record. With an index, it is the record corresponding to the last index entry. After the SKIP *n* command, the data base is not positioned at any valid record; the RECNO() function evaluates to a number one greater than the number of records in the file, and all fields have blank values. EOF() is also set to .T. if a FIND or SEEK command fails to find the specified record or if a data base accessed through a SET RELATION command has no record that matches the key expression on which the RELATION is based.

ERROR()

Input: None
Output: Number

Evaluates to a number corresponding to the error that has just occurred. This function always returns 0 unless an error trapping routine has been established with the ON ERROR command. The ERROR() function may be used to detect and respond to certain recoverable error conditions, such as a missing file or, in a network environment, an attempt to lock a record currently being modified by another user.

▶ EXP(<*number*>)

Input: Numeric expression
Output: Number

Evaluates to the result of raising e (the base for natural logarithms) to the power specified by the numeric expression.

▶ FIELD(<*number*>)

Input: Numeric expression
Output: Character string

Evaluates to a character string containing the name of the field specified by number in the data base open in the current work area or a null string if there is no corresponding field in the current data base. This function may be used to determine the number of fields in a data base or to handle a series of fields as an array.

▶ FILE(<*file name*>)

Input: Character expression
Output: Logical value

Evaluates to .T. if the specified file is present on the disk. If the file name is a literal character string (not a memory variable), it must be enclosed in quotation marks. This function may be used to test for the existence of a file before attempting to use it, so that a program may take the appropriate corrective action (creating the file or informing the user) if the file is missing.

▪ ▶ FKLABEL(<*number*>)

Input: Numeric expression
Output: Character string

Evaluates to a character string containing the name of the programmable function key specified by number. Unless the keyboard has a separate HELP key, the meaning of the first function key (usually labelled F1) cannot be reassigned, and FKLABEL(1) returns the name of the second function key. This function may be used to change the meanings of the function keys without having to know their names.

▪ ▶ FKMAX()

Input: None
Output: Number

Evaluates to the number of programmable function keys on the keyboard. Unless the keyboard has a separate HELP key, FKMAX() evaluates to a number one fewer than the actual number of keys. This function may be used to test for the existence of certain function keys before attempting to reassign their meanings.

▪ ▶ FLOCK()

Input: None
Output: Logical value

Evaluates to .T. if it is possible to lock the file that is open in the currently selected work area, or .F. if the attempt fails because the file is already locked by another user. This function simultaneously tests the status and attempts to lock the file. Once locked, the file may be unlocked with the UNLOCK command, by closing the file, or by exiting from dBASE III PLUS. A file is generally locked for operations that affect the entire file or update many records.

▪ ▶ FOUND()

Input: None
Output: Logical value

Evaluates to .T. when a FIND, SEEK, LOCATE, or CONTINUE command positions the record pointer at a valid record in the data base in the current work area or when the record pointer is repositioned automatically to a valid record in a data base in another work area linked to the current file with SET RELATION. In general, when EOF() is .T., FOUND() is .F. dBASE III PLUS keeps track of the value of the FOUND() function separately in each work area, but a work area must be selected to display or operate on this value.

▪ ▶ GETENV(<*character string*>)

Input: Character string expression
Output: Character string

Evaluates to a character string containing the operating system environment parameter specified as input or a null string if the parameter has not been set.

▶ IIF(<condition>, <expression 1>, <expression 2>)

Input: Logical expression, expression, expression
Output: Same data type as expression 1 and 2

Evaluates to expression 1 if the condition is .T. or expression 2 if the condition is .F. The two expressions may be of any data type, but they must be of the same data type. This function is most useful for displaying fields conditionally at the dot prompt and printing fields conditionally in reports and labels, where you cannot use an IF . . . ELSE . . . ENDIF structure.

▶ INKEY()

Input: None
Output: Number

Evaluates to a number corresponding to the key pressed by the operator or the first key in the keyboard buffer if there is more than one. Unlike the WAIT command, using the INKEY() function does not pause the currently running program. Because the function returns a value of 0 unless a key is pressed at the instant it is evaluated, it is generally used within a DO WHILE loop that monitors the keyboard and registers the user's keypress.

▶ INT(<*number*>)

Input: Numeric expression
Output: Number

Evaluates to the integer portion of the number represented by the numeric expression (the result of dropping any digits beyond the decimal point). To round off a number to the nearest integer, use the ROUND function instead.

▪ ▶ ISALPHA(<*character string*>)

Input: Character string expression
Output: Logical value

Evaluates to .T. if the first character of the expression providing the input is a letter of the alphabet or .F. if it is not.

▪ ▶ ISCOLOR()

Input: None
Output: Logical value

Evaluates to .T. if the system is using a color/graphics monitor or .F. if the display is a monochrome screen. This function may be used to detect which type of monitor is present and set the display attributes accordingly. The color selections should be made with caution, however, since not every color/graphics system can actually display colors. For example, the Compaq display returns a .T. value.

▪ ▶ ISLOWER(<*character string*>)

Input: Character string expression
Output: Logical value

Evaluates to .T. if the first character of the expression providing the input is a lowercase letter of the alphabet or .F. if it is not.

▪ ▶ ISUPPER(<*character string*>)

Input: Character string expression
Output: Logical value

Evaluates to .T. if the first character of the expression providing the input is an uppercase letter of the alphabet or .F. if it is not.

▶ LEFT(<*character string*>, <*length*>)

Input: Character string expression, numeric expression
Output: Character string

Evaluates to a substring (part of a string) of the character string represented by the expression providing the input. The substring begins with the first (left-most) character and the length is specified by the numeric expression. If the requested length exceeds the length of the original character string, the substring consists of the full string.

▪ ► LEN(<*character string*>)

Input: Character string expression
Output: Number

Evaluates to the length of the character string represented by the character string expression. The length of a data base field is always the full field width. The TRIM function may be used to eliminate trailing blanks.

▪ ► LOCK() or RLOCK()

Input: None
Output: Logical value

Evaluates to .T. if it is possible to lock the current record in the data base open in the current work area or .F. if the record is already locked by another user. This function simultaneously tests the status and attempts to lock the record. Once locked, the record may be unlocked with the UNLOCK command. This function is generally used for operations that involve updating records one at a time, so that multiple users may access the same file, but not the same record, at the same time.

► LOG(<*number*>)

Input: Numeric expression
Output: Number

Evaluates to the natural (base e) logarithm of the number represented by the numeric expression.

▶ LOWER(<*character string*>)

Input: Character string expression
Output: Character string

Evaluates to the result of converting the character string represented by the character string expression to all lowercase. This function may be used to convert a character string entered in various mixtures of uppercase and lowercase to a consistent format for comparison to another variable or constant.

▶ LTRIM(<*character string*>)

Input: Character string expression
Output: Character string

Evaluates to a character string consisting of the result of evaluating the specified character string expression, with all leading blanks removed. This function is useful for removing leading blanks created when a numeric expression is converted to a character string with the STR function.

▶ LUPDATE()

Input: None
Output: Date

Evaluates to the date the data base in the current work area was last updated by adding, changing, or deleting data.

▶ MAX(<*numeric expression*>, <*numeric expression*>)

Input: Numeric expression, numeric expression
Output: Number

Evaluates to the number represented by the greater of the two numeric expressions. This function is useful for displaying fields conditionally at the dot prompt and printing fields conditionally in reports and labels, where you cannot use an IF . . . ELSE . . . ENDIF structure to select the greater value.

▪ ▶ MESSAGE()

Input: None
Output: Character string

Evaluates to a character string containing the error message normally displayed by dBASE III PLUS in response to the error that has just occurred. This function always returns 0 unless an error trapping routine has been established with the ON ERROR command.

▶ MIN(<*numeric expression*>, <*numeric expression*>)

Input: Numeric expression, numeric expression
Output: Number

Evaluates to the number represented by the smaller of the two numeric expressions. This function is useful for displaying fields conditionally at the dot prompt and printing fields conditionally in reports and labels, where you cannot use an IF . . . ELSE . . . ENDIF structure to select the smaller value.

MOD(<*numeric expression*>, <*numeric expression*>)

Input: Numeric expression, numeric expression
Output: Number

Evaluates to the remainder that results from dividing the first numeric expression by the second.

MONTH(<*date*>)

Input: Date expression
Output: Number

Evaluates to a number representing the month in the specified date.

NDX(<*numeric expression*>)

Input: Numeric expression
Output: Character string

Evaluates to a character string consisting of the full name (or path name, if the file is not in the current subdirectory) of the index file whose position in the index file list specified in the USE command that opened the data base in the current work area corresponds to the value of the numeric expression or to a null string if no such index is open.

▪ ▶ OS()

Input: None
Output: Character string

Evaluates to a character string containing the name of the operating system currently running. This function may be used to determine which operating system is active before using the RUN command to run an external command or program specific to a particular operating system.

▪ ▶ PCOL()

Input: None
Output: Number

Evaluates to a number representing the current print head column position. This function may be used to print data immediately following the last item printed or a fixed number of columns to the right of the last item, without reference to the absolute print head position.

▪ ▶ PROW()

Input: None
Output: Number

Evaluates to a number representing the current print head row position. This function may be used to print data on the next available row (line) on the page or a fixed number of rows below this row, without reference to the absolute print head position.

READKEY()

Input: None
Output: Number

Evaluates to a number corresponding to the key pressed by the operator to exit from any full-screen edit mode, including a series of @ . . . SAY . . . GET commands followed by a READ. Each key can generate two possible values, depending on whether or not data was changed during the full-screen edit process.

RECCOUNT()

Input: None
Output: Number

Evaluates to the number of records in the data base open in the currently selected work area.

RECNO()

Input: None
Output: Number

Evaluates to the record number at the position of the record pointer in the data base open in the currently selected work area. If the data base is positioned past the end-of-file, RECNO() evaluates to one greater than the number of records in the file. This means that if the data base is empty, RECNO() has the value 1.

▶ RECSIZE()

Input: None
Output: Number

Evaluates to the record length of the data base in the currently selected work area. This function may be combined with the RECCOUNT () function to calculate the approximate size of a data base (not including the space occupied by the file header).

▶ REPLICATE(<*character string*>, <*number*>)

Input: Character string expression, numeric expression
Output: Character string

Evaluates to a character string consisting of the character string specified as input, repeated a number of times equal to the value of the numeric expression.

▶ RIGHT(<*character string*>, <*length*>)

Input: Character string expression, numeric expression
Output: Character string

Evaluates to a substring (part of a string) of the character string represented by the expression providing the input. The length of the substring is specified by the numeric expression, and the substring is taken from the right side of the original string. If the requested length exceeds the length of the original character string, the substring consists of the full string.

RLOCK() or LOCK()

Input: None
Output: Logical value

RLOCK() is identical to LOCK() and is provided for parity with the FLOCK() function.

ROUND(<*number*>, <*decimals*>)

Input: Numeric expression, numeric expression
Output: Number

The result of rounding off the number represented by the first numeric expression to the number of decimal places specified by the second. If *decimals* is a negative number, the specified number of digits to the *left* of the decimal point are rounded off.

ROW()

Input: None
Output: Number

Evaluates to a number representing the current cursor row position on the screen. This function may be used to display data on the next available row (line) on the screen or a fixed number of rows away from this row, without reference to the absolute cursor position.

▶ RTRIM(<*character string*>)

Input: Character string expression
Output: Character string

RTRIM is identical to TRIM and is provided for parity with the LTRIM function.

▶ SPACE(<*number*>)

Input: Numeric expression
Output: Character string

Evaluates to a character string consisting of the number of blank spaces specified by the numeric expression. This function is often used to initialize a blank character memory variable without having to count spaces.

▶ SQRT(<*number*>)

Input: Numeric expression
Output: Number

Evaluates to the square root of the number represented by the numeric expression.

▶ STR(<*number*> [,<*length*>] [,<*decimals*>])

Input: Numeric expression, numeric expression, numeric expression
Output: Character string

Evaluates to a character string representation of the number specified by the first numeric expression.

The length of the string is specified by the second expression, and the number of decimal places by the third. If the length is omitted, it is assumed to be 10. If you do not specify the number of decimal places, 0 is assumed. This function may be used to convert a number to a character string so that it may be concatenated with another character string for display, printing, or use in an index key expression.

▶ STUFF(<*character string 1*>, <*starting position*>, <*length*>, <*character string 2*>)

Input: Character string expression, numeric expression, numeric expression, character string

Output: Character string

Evaluates to a character string consisting of the string represented by character string 1, with a substring of the specified length and starting at the indicated starting position removed and replaced by character string 2. If the length is 0, no characters are removed before the substitution is made, and, if character string 2 is a null string, no replacement is made.

▶ SUBSTR(<*character string*>, <*starting position*> [,<*length*>])

Input: Character string expression, numeric expression, numeric expression

Output: Character string

Evaluates to the substring (part of a string) of the

specified character string that begins at the position represented by the first numeric expression. If a second numeric expression is included, it specifies the length of the substring. If the length is omitted, the substring begins at the designated starting position and includes all of the remaining characters in the original string.

▶ TIME()

Input: None
Output: Character string

Evaluates to a character string representation of the current system time.

▶ TRANSFORM(<*expression*>, <*picture*>)

Input: Expression, character string expression
Output: Same data type as expression

Evaluates to the result of formatting the expression with the specified PICTURE. This function may be used to format fields displayed from the dot prompt and to print formatted data in reports and labels. The data type of the output is the same as the data type of the original expression; however, you cannot accumulate column totals and subtotals in a report printed by the built-in report generator for any numeric fields formatted with this function.

▶ TRIM(<*character string*>)

Input: Character string expression
Output: Character string

Evaluates to a character string consisting of the result of evaluating the specified character string expression, with all trailing blanks removed. This function is identical to RTRIM.

▶ TYPE(<*expression*>)

Input: Any expression
Output: Character

Evaluates to a single character representing the data type of the specified expression, for a character (C), numeric (N), logical (L), or memo (M) expression (date type expressions are not permitted as input). If a variable does not exist or if the expression is not syntactically correct, the function evaluates to U (undefined). To use this function to test for the existence of a variable, the variable name supplied as input must be enclosed in quotation marks; otherwise, the *content* of the variable is evaluated, not the variable itself.

▶ UPPER(<*character string*>)

Input: Character string expression
Output: Character string

Evaluates to the result of converting the specified character string expression to all uppercase. This function may be used to convert a character string entered in various mixtures of uppercase and lowercase to a consistent format for comparison to another variable or constant.

▶ VAL(<*character string*>)

Input: Character string expression
Output: Number

Evaluates to a true number matching the character string representation of the number supplied as input.

▪ ▶ VERSION()

Input: None
Output: Character string

Evaluates to a character string containing the name of the version of dBASE III PLUS that is running. This function may be used to test the version of dBASE III PLUS before issuing a command or using a function not present in an older version.

▶ YEAR(<*date*>)

Input: Date expression
Output: Number

Evaluates to a four-digit number representing the year in the specified date.

THE CONFIG.DB FILE

The CONFIG.DB file is a configuration file used to customize the status of the dBASE III PLUS working environment to suit your personal preferences. CONFIG.DB is an ASCII text file consisting of one or more command lines, each of which controls one option. If this file is present in the subdirectory from which you load dBASE III PLUS, or a subdirectory specified in a DOS PATH command, the settings it contains are automatically placed in effect when you start up the program.

Most of the options you may specify in CONFIG.DB may also be established with SET commands; these are described in the alphabetical command reference. The eight options that may *not* be SET from the dot prompt govern the use of external word processors and the allocation of RAM for memory buffers, which must be known to dBASE III PLUS when the program is first loaded. These options are marked with an asterisk (*) and explained below.

There are no CONFIG.DB equivalents for SET commands that require a data base to be open, such as SET FIELDS and SET FILTER, as well as several others: SET DATE, SET DOHISTORY, SET FIXED, SET MESSAGE, SET PRINTER, and SET TITLE.

The syntax used in CONFIG.DB is different from the syntax of the corresponding SET options.

The general format for a CONFIG.DB entry is:

<option> = *<value>*

instead of

SET *<option>* *<value>*

or

SET *<option>* TO *<value>*

The default values of options with two or more alternate values (for example, ON or OFF) are indicated in upper case.

ALTERNATE = ***<file name>***

This command is equivalent to the two SET commands

SET ALTERNATE TO *<file name>*
SET ALTERNATE ON

BELL = **ON/off**

* **BUCKET** = ***<number>***

This option specifies the amount of memory (expressed in kilobytes) reserved by dBASE III PLUS for PICTURE, FUNCTION, and RANGE clauses in @ . . . SAY . . . GET commands. The default is 2, and you may specify any number between 1 and 31. This number should be increased if you experience inexplicable problems with @ . . . SAY . . . GET commands.

CARRY = **on/OFF**

CATALOG = ***<file name>***

CENTURY = **on/OFF**

COLOR = ***<standard foreground/standard background>, <enhanced foreground/ enhanced background>, <border>***

* **COMMAND** = ***<command>***

The specified command is run automatically when you first load dBASE III PLUS.The default CONFIG.DB file provided with dBASE III PLUS contains the line COMMAND = ASSIST so that the program starts up in ASSIST mode. The COMMAND command is often used to run the main menu program in a dBASE III PLUS application. If the user invokes a different command file when loading dBASE III PLUS by typing DBASE *<program name>*, it overrides the CONFIG.DB entry.

CONFIRM = **on/OFF**

CONSOLE = **ON/off**

DEBUG = **on/OFF**

DECIMALS = ***<number>***

DEFAULT = ***<disk drive>***

DELETED = **on/OFF**

* **DELIMITERS** = ***<delimiter character(s)>***

The delimiter characters must *not* be enclosed in quotes, as they are in the equivalent SET command.

DELIMITERS = **on/OFF**

DEVICE = **SCREEN/print**

ECHO = **on/OFF**

ENCRYPTION = **ON/off**

ESCAPE = **ON/off**

EXACT = **on/OFF**

EXCLUSIVE = **ON/off**

F<*number*> = **<*character string*>**
This is equivalent to SET FUNCTION.

FIXED = **on/OFF**

* **GETS** = **<*number*>**
This option determines the number of GETs that may be collected between READ, CLEAR GETS, or CLEAR commands. The default is 128, and you may specify any number between 35 and 1023.

HEADING = **ON/off**

HELP = **ON/off**

HISTORY = **<*number*>**

INTENSITY = **ON/off**

MARGIN = **<*number*>**

* **MAXMEM** = **<*number*>**
This option determines the amount of memory (expressed in kilobytes) that is not released by dBASE III PLUS to an external application executed with a RUN command. The default value is 256, and you may specify any number between 200 and 720. MAXMEM should be raised if you have increased the amount of memory used by

dBASE III PLUS by increasing the values of MVARSIZ, GETS, or BUCKET, so that these necessary memory buffers are not overwritten when external programs or commands are executed.

MEMOWIDTH = ***<number>***

MENUS = **ON/off**

* **MVARSIZ** = ***<number>***
This option specifies the amount of memory (expressed in kilobytes) reserved by dBASE III PLUS for memory variables. The default is 6, and you may specify any number between 1 and 31.

PATH = ***<path name list>***

PRINT = **on/OFF**

PRINTER = ***<DOS device name>***

* **PROMPT** = ***<character string>***
This option changes the dBASE III PLUS command prompt from the standard dot (.) to the specified character string.

SAFETY = **ON/off**

SCOREBOARD = **ON/off**

STATUS = **ON/off**

STEP = **on/OFF**

TALK = **ON/off**

* **TEDIT** = ***<file name>***
This option specifies an external text editor or word processing program that is substituted for

the standard dBASE III PLUS MODIFY COMMAND editor. The file name should be entered exactly as you would type it at the MS-DOS prompt to invoke the editor (it must not include an extension).

TYPEAHEAD = ***<number>***

UNIQUE = **on/OFF**

VIEW = ***<file name>***

* **WP** = ***<file name>***

This option specifies an external text editor or word processing program that is substituted for the standard dBASE III PLUS memo field editor. The file name should be entered exactly as you would type it at the MS-DOS prompt to invoke the editor (it must not include an extension).